How to Organize Yourself

CREATING SUCCESS
SERIES

The above titles are available from all good bookshops.

For further information on these and other Kogan Page titles, or to order online, visit www.koganpage.com.

Seventh edition

How to Organize Yourself

Simple ways to take control,
save time and work more efficiently

John Caunt

First published in Great Britain and the United States in 2000 by Kogan Page Limited as *Organize Yourself*
Fourth edition published in 2013 as *How to Organize Yourself*
Seventh edition 2022

2nd Floor, 45 Gee Street	8 W 38th Street, Suite 902	4737/23 Ansari Road
London	New York, NY 10018	Daryaganj
EC1V 3RS	USA	New Delhi 110002
United Kingdom		India
www.koganpage.com		

© John Caunt, 2000, 2006, 2010, 2013, 2016, 2019, 2022

ISBNs
Hardback   978 1 3986 0632 6
Paperback   978 1 3986 0609 8
Ebook   978 1 3986 0633 3

British Library Cataloguing-in-Publication Data
A CIP record for this book is available from the British Library.

Library of Congress Cataloging-in-Publication Control Number
Names: Caunt, John, author.
Title: How to organize yourself: simple ways to take control, save time and work more efficiently / John Caunt.
Description: Seventh edition. | London, United Kingdom; New York, NY: Kogan Page, 2022. | Series: Creating success series
Identifiers: LCCN 2022008073 (print) | LCCN 2022008074 (ebook) | ISBN 9781398606098 (paperback) | ISBN 9781398606326 (hardback) | ISBN 9781398606333 (ebook)
Subjects: LCSH: Time management. | Personal information management. | Life skills.
Classification: LCC HD69.T54 C39 2022 (print) | LCC HD69.T54 (ebook) | DDC 650.1/1–dc23/eng/20220222
LC record available at https://lccn.loc.gov/2022008073
LC ebook record available at https://lccn.loc.gov/2022008074

Typeset by Hong Kong FIVE Workshop
Print production managed by Jellyfish
Printed and bound by CPI Group (UK) Ltd, Croydon CR0 4YY

CONTENTS

Introduction

Never have we experienced a greater need to be organized. The working environment of today is characterized by constantly rising pressure to deliver with fewer resources. Against a background of restructuring and cost-cutting we are expected to keep a larger number of balls in the air and to do so with less support. The picture is increasingly one of self-sufficient professionals responsible for all aspects of their workplace organization. The information age provides us with tools to organize our working lives, but it also presents us with many challenges in the form of increased volumes of information, constant connectedness, expectations of immediacy, and interruptions to our routines.

Outside our working lives, we have greater expectations of our leisure time, and we readily expect to be able to fulfil family commitments while we and our partners hold down demanding jobs. We juggle the different elements of our lives to cram in trips and excursions, duty visits, entertainment, house-keeping, health pursuits, personal development, voluntary responsibilities, family activities and time with friends.

To cope with all of this we need to be organized. We need to handle time, information, people and technology as efficiently and effectively as possible in order to deliver the results on which we will be judged. Being organized means:

- less time spent firefighting and responding to crises;
- sharper focus on the things that matter most in terms of producing results;
- the ability to see your way through complex problems and challenges;
- more time for family, friends and leisure;

- reduced stress and fatigue;
- greater sense of achievement;
- the chance to step back and take pride in a job well done.

Even though the benefits of greater organization are clear, we present ourselves with excuses for failing to acquire them:

> Excuse 1 – 'The ability to be organized is something innate. It's a quality that you either possess or lack, and I just don't have it.'

Certainly it's true that we vary in our natural tendency towards being organized, but it isn't true that there is nothing we can do to overcome that inclination. Ever since the 1960s there has been a tendency within popular psychology to associate certain traits with a dominant role for one or other of the two brain hemispheres – the left being judged superior for analytical functioning and the right for more creative tasks. Numerous questionnaires, inventories and personality profiles have reinforced the notion that attributes such as being organized are part of the way we are wired up, and that left-brain or right-brain dominance are fixed behaviour-determining features. But recent research has suggested such rigid categorization is erroneous, and revealed that all parts of the brain are engaged in activities that had previously been attributed to one or the other hemisphere. It's true you may not have a natural inclination towards being organized and methodical, but that just means you have to work a little harder at acquiring the necessary skills. And just in case you are wondering, I'll own up now to being a person who has to work quite hard at being organized.

> Excuse 2 – 'There is no way that I could be organized in my workplace. The constant interruptions, the crises, the disorganized colleagues.'

Yes, there are plenty of workplaces where it is hard to be organized, but that is no reason to give up. In the chapters that follow we will look at how you can take control of your working environment to reduce interruptions and distractions, and we'll consider how good planning and effective delegation can help forestall crises and minimize colleague dependency.

Excuse 3 – 'I would like to be more organized but I'm just too busy to spend time on it at the moment. Perhaps in a couple of months' time.'

In today's work climate, the person who postpones action in the hope of having more time a month, two months, six months from now, is destined to be forever disappointed. And what does 'being too busy' really mean? It is possible to spend your working days scurrying in every direction and achieving little – you may be busy but not effective. Targeted activity is what brings results, and improved organization is largely about targeting your activity.

For many of us the aim of becoming more organized has a great deal in common with those other ubiquitous lifestyle objectives – getting fit or losing weight. We believe it will be good for us and our lives will be fuller and more satisfying if we can accomplish it, but somehow we never seem to achieve it to the degree or with the consistency we seek. In the same way as we embark on successive diets and fitness programmes, so we pitch ourselves into organizational splurges that may bear fruit for a while before we sink back into our depressingly chaotic old ways. We latch onto some new regime or rush to acquire the piece of equipment or software that we believe will solve our organizational problems for us. And perhaps, for a time, it seems to do the trick. But then we lose our focus, the old habits start to reappear, systems go down the tubes and procrastination is the order of the day.

It doesn't have to be like that. Everyone can become more organized – and not just for a month or three months, but permanently. However, there's no instant fix – sustainable change requires more than a new gadget or a few quick tips. It requires attention to your current attitudes and expectations, a degree of perseverance in building new routines, and readiness to pull together all the threads – time, information, people and technology – to produce a package of actions that will work for you.

So, if you have made previous attempts at better organization that haven't worked out, don't despair. You can do it, and I hope this book will provide you with many of the strategies needed to get you there. But don't adopt everything I suggest religiously: be prepared to adapt or experiment with what is written here and build a system that is not mine, but yours.

Whilst most of the examples used in this book are work related, the principles and strategies suggested are just as applicable to those seeking to bring better organization into their home, leisure or voluntary activity. Nor, from a work point of view, should it be assumed that there is any perceived target audience in terms of occupational groups or levels of workforce seniority. The pressures of the modern workplace are fairly universal, and the steps to improved personal organization are pretty much the same whatever your job. There will be differences, of course, in the volumes and nature of information you are required to handle, the amount of support you are able to call upon and the number of colleagues, clients and contacts you have to relate to. But whether you are a newly appointed junior, an established professional or a self- employed homeworker, there is something here for you.

In those sections that deal with aspects of technology, it is assumed that most readers will have some familiarity with computers and other digital devices, but that their knowledge may be piecemeal. The speed of technological advance and the proliferation of electronic devices and applications mean that detailed and up-to-date coverage of available options is impossible in a short book such as this. However, I have used as examples some of the most popular or well-regarded applications at the time of writing.

01
Know where you are going

This book contains information on a whole range of techniques, technology and tips to assist with your personal organization, but none will do the trick without the first essential ingredient. That is you and your approach to the process of becoming more organized. The first step to being organized occurs not in the latest smartphone app or killer piece of software but in your head. If you are to take control of your life and begin to make a difference, you must address your organizational weaknesses and strengths, the reasons for current disorganization and your attitude towards changing the situation. You should ensure too that you have a clear idea of where you are heading and how you expect to get there.

We all have our organizational strengths and weaknesses, so before going any further take a moment to ask yourself where your particular shortcomings lie. Which of the following statements apply to you?

- 'There is a lack of overall direction to my work.'
- 'I have difficulty extracting priorities from the mass of tasks and issues that come my way.'
- 'My days seem to slip away with little achieved.'
- 'I don't plan my time adequately.'
- 'I end the day with more items on my 'to do' list than I started with.'
- 'I find it hard to estimate how long some tasks are going to take.'

- 'Deadlines seem to creep up on me.'
- 'I'm not sure that I make best use of the times when my energy levels are highest.'
- 'I flit in and out of routine tasks, often letting them interrupt more important work.'
- 'I tend to postpone tasks I don't like.'
- 'Trivial tasks assume greater importance than they should.'
- 'I would like to be more systematic in my decision making.'
- 'I spend huge amounts of time dealing with email.'
- 'I don't often tackle messages and documents when I first look at them.'
- 'I am often unable to decide what to do with information I receive.'
- 'I would like to assimilate documents more quickly.'
- 'I forget a lot of what I read.'
- 'I find myself attending too many unproductive meetings.'
- 'I don't think I delegate enough.'
- 'Colleagues bombard me with information I don't need.'
- 'I am plagued by interruptions.'
- 'Too often I take on tasks I should refuse.'
- 'My workspace layout isn't conducive to good organization.'
- 'There are piles of paper in my office, my desk is cluttered and my files are disorganized.'
- 'My computer desktop is chaotic and files are inadequately labelled.'
- 'I spend a lot of time looking for things.'
- 'I am concerned that I am not adequately utilizing technology to organize my work.'
- 'I don't use the internet as effectively as I might.'
- 'My personal organization declines when I am working from home.'

Reasons for disorganization

The preceding checklist aims to help you identify some of your current organizational weaknesses, but it's useful also to explore the reasons for them. In broad terms we could say there are three main drivers of disorganization: external pressures, systems failures and personal factors. The first includes such things as overload, interruptions and problems with the working environment, while the second relates to absence of strategies and routines for managing time and information, and failure to use tools appropriately. It is the third area that we most often neglect. Personal factors affecting disorganization might include anxiety about certain tasks or a desire for novelty that leads us to flit from one task to another. Also present might be a tendency towards perfectionism, a habit of taking on too much, an unwillingness to delegate or a failure to say no on occasions. All of these problems can be tackled, but first they need to be recognized, so take a moment now to ask yourself the following question.

Activity – ask yourself

What are the main reasons I am less organized than I would wish to be? Jot down your responses under these headings:

- external pressures;
- lack of suitable strategies and routines;
- personal factors.

Your answers will be useful in an objective setting activity later in the chapter.

Attitudes towards organizing

Disorganization is not, in the main, something about which we feel a sense of shame. In fact we can present it to ourselves as almost an endearing quality – an indication that there is more to us than boring routines, rigid attention to maintaining schedules or an obsessive desire to ensure that everything is in its proper place. As long as we persist in such attitudes, we are likely to hold some inner resistance to becoming more organized, and the changes we seek will be more difficult.

In the Introduction I presented some of the excuses we give ourselves for not becoming more organized, but sometimes there are more than just excuses. We may have entrenched beliefs about ourselves that hold us back even when we have decided to act. Beliefs such as these can lead us to doubt our ability to change:

- 'I've been like this so long I'm not sure I can change my ways.'
- 'I'm just naturally untidy.'
- 'I'm so easily distracted – can't keep my attention on anything for long.'

One way to shift such unhelpful beliefs is to search out contrary evidence. Take a good look at your life and the likelihood is you will be able to find areas where you are organized. Perhaps good organization is apparent in some leisure interest to which you are able to give time and attention despite your otherwise busy schedule. Maybe it occurs in aspects of your domestic arrangements. Even in areas of your life where chaos appears to rule, there will be pockets of good organization – items that are stored where you are always able to put your hands on them and routines that get the job done quickly and effectively. What is it about these aspects of your work or your life that has made them different? Are there features of your organizational successes that you can transfer into other elements of your life? Focus on the things that are working well in addition to those that are not, and use them to build a more positive view of the way forward. Have a go now at listing your strengths, in whatever area of your life they are to be found. Writing them down will generally add to the value of the exercise.

Don't just confine yourself to consideration of strengths that are overtly to do with the detail of organization. Other more general attributes can also play their part. Consider such qualities as adaptability, resilience, patience, determination, self-control, analytical abilities, creativity, curiosity, perceptiveness and versatility. It's almost invariably possible to unearth additional characteristics that can play their part in helping you become more organized and these, along with overlooked instances of organized behaviour, will offer a foundation for overcoming your identified weaknesses.

Even if you are still struggling to find strengths you may deploy, you shouldn't despair. A proven method of building the attributes you need is to 'fake it until you make it'. This isn't about pretending to others, but of determining that you will practise and perfect the desired characteristics in the interests of your own self-belief and progress. And it does work. As Aristotle wrote: 'Whatever we learn to do, we learn by actually doing it: men come to be builders, for instance, by building, and harp players by playing the harp. In the same way, by doing just acts, we come to be just; by doing self-controlled acts, we come to be self-controlled; and by doing brave acts, we become brave.'

If you are to remove unhelpful attitudes towards organization, it is also important to weed out any negative self-talk. Statements like 'I'm never able to muscle down to tasks', whether made privately to yourself or shared in conversation with others, only serve to reinforce a sense of helplessness. Replace them with positive affirmations – simple and strong but realistic statements repeated regularly to yourself: 'I can achieve everything I set out to do.' 'I can handle interruptions and get back on track.' 'I can change disorganized habits.' 'I can cope with whatever the day throws at me.' Choose some affirmations that are right for you and mentally repeat these statements of faith in yourself on a regular basis.

I wouldn't want to exaggerate the importance of affirmations. Provided they are sensible and realistic, they represent a useful tool for changing negative attitudes, but they are not the magic bullet that some positive-thinking exponents would have you believe.

It's essential too that you shift any attitudes that may reinforce the notion that organization is a wholly tedious process or that disorganized people are somehow more interesting than their more organized colleagues. Visualize the benefits of a better-organized life style. How will it feel? What will better organization offer you that you don't have at present?

Visualizing the benefits of greater organization is made easier if you have a clear view of what your objectives actually are, but in a busy, multifaceted life this may be more easily said than done. You may have a host of vaguely articulated goals, commitments and aspirations. Some will overlap; some may conflict. There will be those that you have originated and others over which you have little control. They may be associated with any of the elements that constitute your life: work, leisure activities, family and relation-ships, voluntary responsibilities, learning and development.

To assist in clarifying your thoughts, let me ask you a simple question that should help identify some of the things that are important to you.

Why do I want to be more organized?

Ask yourself that question now. Jot down all the answers that come to mind and follow any trail that an answer generates.

Example

Q: Why do I want to be more organized?

A: So that I can get more done during my working week.

How will that benefit me?

- It will mean less need to take work home at evenings and weekends.
- It will mean more time to spend with the people I care about.
- It will free me up to engage in new sporting and leisure interests.
- It will demonstrate to others that I'm on top of my job.
- It may show that I'm worthy of promotion.
- It could lead to a greater sense of job satisfaction.

Pursuing this question helps to shift the sort of negative attitudes I was referring to earlier and reinforces the point that the changes you are seeking are not ends in themselves, but means to achieving those things that are really important in your work and your life in general.

An understanding of broad aims is an important starting point to becoming more organized. But the next essential step is to identify the practical things that will have to be accomplished if you are to achieve those aims, and that means giving some attention to setting objectives. Let's take a look at objective setting now.

Setting objectives

Whether you are thinking about major life goals, the requirements of a work project or the process of becoming more organized, time spent determining your objectives is more than likely to be repaid. Unfortunately, objective setting is often hedged around with a certain amount of jargon and mystique that can deter the uninitiated. But it doesn't have to be a big deal. An objective is just a tool, the purpose of which is to transform amorphous challenges into tasks you can get your teeth into and that will lead to meaningful outcomes. It needs to be clear and precise, but don't go overboard in your search for complete precision. An objective that is a little loose is better than no objective at all. This is particularly the case when you are setting objectives for yourself rather than for others. You know what you mean; others might not.

Try to produce objectives that are SMART – specific, measurable, achievable, results oriented and time related.

Specific

The more general an objective, the harder it is to focus on those tasks and activities necessary to bring about its achievement. As an example let's consider your purpose in reading this book. You're doing it because you want to become more organized. That's OK as a general aim but it's not much help in getting to where you want to be. For that, you need to break your general aim down into objectives that are more specific in terms of the things you are going to do. The specifics are those things you may already have identified as weaknesses to be resolved – for example, overcoming procrastination, clarifying priorities or eliminating clutter.

Measurable

Without a measurable element to your objectives you have no way of determining at what point they have been achieved, and the resultant vagueness may mean a loss of focus. You might decide, for example, that one of your objectives in respect of personal organization is to improve your keyboard input speed. But what constitutes successful achievement – an improvement of one word per minute, or an improvement of 30? Only with some idea of scale does the objective have precision. And don't neglect the fact that there may need to be more than one measurable element if an objective is to have any value. An increase in typing speed of 30 words a minute may be entirely achievable but at a cost to accuracy that renders the improvement meaningless. Whilst you may be prepared to sacrifice some degree of accuracy in the initial drive towards increasing performance, you will want to ensure that such losses are recovered later on. However, don't be too rigid or arbitrary in the measurable elements you introduce to your objectives. Excessive quantification may actually hamper achievement as attention spent on measuring gets in the way of what is being measured. And lack of flexibility may mean that you hit a brick wall when unforeseen obstacles appear, or may even lead you to ignore opportunities for further development beyond the stated target.

Achievable

Any objective you set should be achievable. The reason you are using the objective is in order to get things done and to obtain the positive reinforcement that comes from success. It is not the purpose of objectives to add unnecessary stress to your life and deliver the negative reinforcement of failure. On the other hand, there is little to be gained by setting objectives that can be achieved with minimal effort. You may get a slight buzz when you cross them off your list of things to do, but deep down you won't be fooled by the illusion of progress. The trick is to set immediate objectives that are just out of reach. It's a matter of having to stretch yourself to achieve them, but not to saddle yourself with aspirations that will be impossible to meet.

Does that mean that you can't have a grand objective – a target that is well beyond your current capabilities? No, it doesn't, provided that you break down your main objectives into sub-goals and work towards your grand vision in manageable steps.

You might, for example, have a grand objective of reducing the weekly hours you spend on work matters from a current average of 55 to an average of 40, while maintaining current levels of output and quality. This is most probably a target that will require attention to many of the elements covered in this book, and should be broken down into sub-goals, each with realistic stages towards achievement. One such sub-goal might concern improved ability to delegate. But within this there needs to be recognition that the early stages of such a process might actually mean an investment of more time, as you give attention to such activities as identifying those tasks it is possible to delegate, briefing the people who will take them on and working to ensure that the tasks are perceived as valuable and challenging. Your staged objectives should take account of this time investment and provide the space for it before the time savings start to kick in.

Results oriented

Objectives should be described in terms of results delivered rather than activities. If, as part of a drive to become more organized, you determine that you will arrive at work an hour earlier in the mornings, this simply describes the activity. You can spend that hour drinking coffee and chatting, and you will still meet the objective. A far better objective would include identification of those things you propose to achieve in the hour – possibly the completion of tasks that require uninterrupted concentration and are therefore more difficult to accomplish in the hurly-burly of the regular working day.

Time related

Objectives generally benefit from clear deadlines by which they will be completed. This links closely with the requirement that they be achievable. An objective may be achievable in one timescale but not in another. Deadlines are also helpful in providing motivation and maintaining momentum, provided that they are related to a period of time that you are able to get hold of. A deadline six months hence is too vague and distant for most of us. If we are to maintain consistent effort and motivation for a period of more than a month, then we will generally benefit from breaking our target down into smaller stages – individual weeks or months. This may mean building in monthly milestones – review points on the road to your main goal – or setting a series of sub-goals. If, for example, you conclude that it should be possible over a period of three months to reduce the amount of time you spend in meetings from a current average of 12 hours a week to 6, you might set staged targets of a two hour per week reduction in each month with a specific monthly focus:

- Month 1 – extricate yourself from unnecessary meetings.
- Month 2 – find more time-efficient alternative ways of doing some of the business currently conducted in meetings.
- Month 3 – improve the efficiency of those meetings you remain involved with.

Activity

So far in this chapter you have identified some of your organizational weaknesses as well as personal strengths you might utilize in becoming more organized. You have answered the question 'Why do I want to become more organized?' and you have looked at considerations to be borne in mind when formulating objectives. It's now time to pull all those elements together by articulating a set of objectives in respect of better organization. Write them in the form of a numbered list arranged in order of their importance to you at this time, and taking account of the above SMART points. In some cases, you might already have ideas of sub-goals and the detailed steps you expect to take towards the achievement of each main goal. If so, note these as well, but don't be too concerned about producing a detailed action plan at this stage. You will have the opportunity to refine your objectives as you work through the book, and we will review progress and plan a way forward in the final chapter.

In the previous activity we considered only objectives in relation to better organization. Your direction and effectiveness will benefit from having them across all the main elements of your life and work, but if they don't currently exist in some areas, give yourself adequate time to structure and implement them. Attempting to focus on too many objectives at one time can prove overwhelming. Better to concentrate on priority areas initially and build in additional objectives as you progress.

Balancing the different elements of your life

Your life is made up of a whole variety of elements each competing for your time and attention, and it's easy to be side-tracked into one element to the detriment of others. A particular activity may start to take up more of your attention than anticipated, or an interesting issue may draw you away from other priorities. Take care to focus on the big picture and apportion your limited resources in a balanced way to ensure that you make progress in all aspects of your life – work, leisure and relaxation.

Whatever your job or lifestyle, there is likely to be a range of conflicting demands upon your time. So spend a few moments now considering adjustments you might make to the activities that take up your time and energy.

Activity – ask yourself

1   Are there elements of my life that are currently taking a greater proportion of my time and attention than they should? If so, what are they?

2   Why have they become excessively demanding?

3 What elements of my life should I be spending more time on?

4 What might I do to start adjusting the balance between points 1 and 3?

Try to formulate your answers to point 4 in terms of realistic objectives that you can add to the list you produced earlier.

Determining day-to-day priorities

Life would be easy if, having planned the way forward, we could quietly and systematically pursue the achievement of our objectives. But it's seldom like that. In all probability, your day is spent responding to a multitude of routine chores, crises, requests and interruptions. In the face of this bombardment you need a means of determining which tasks will take priority. A simple way of looking at this is to define every demand upon your time, whether it is self-generated or comes in the form of a request, in terms of its importance and its urgency.

The Second World War general and former US President Dwight Eisenhower was apparently keen on ordering priorities in this way, and reportedly said, 'What is important is seldom urgent and what is urgent is seldom important.' The principle of looking at time demands in terms of importance and urgency was subsequently popularized by Stephen R Covey in his book *The 7 Habits of Highly Effective People*, and has been widely adopted by time-management practitioners. We can use a simple assessment of importance and urgency to categorize any task in one of four ways (see Figure 1.1).

Figure 1.1   Determining priorities

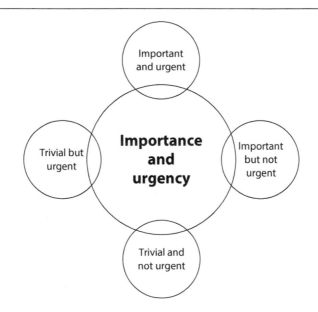

Tasks that are important and urgent

Items that are both important and urgent are clearly the ones to which you must give the most immediate attention, but they are not always instantly identifiable. What constitutes 'important' can be problematic. A manipulative colleague may persuade you that what is important to him or her should feature just as highly on your agenda. Even worse, you may be the guilty party – convincing yourself that a minor diversion is an essential task that simply cannot wait. 'Important' in this context should mean important for the realization of your main objectives – not just those associated with your work, but wider, quality of life objectives too. If a balanced life style and family time have high priority for you, then getting to your child's first end of term concert will rightly be just as important as anything your workplace can throw at you.

It's also worth questioning the notion of urgency. Once again it could be a case of other people's agendas rather than your own.

It might be a matter of urgency that could have been avoided if you had planned your time better or if you had got down to work earlier rather than procrastinating. Some of us do our best work when spurred by a sense of urgency, but urgency that you control – where you set your own deadline or plan to work under time pressure – is a different matter from the sense of crisis and panic that comes from urgency that has crept up on you.

Tasks that are important but not urgent

These are the ones that generally present the biggest problems for those of us whose organization is not as good as it could be. They tend to be concerned with longer term objectives or major life quality issues and we need to ensure that we find the time to progress them. But often we are guilty of ignoring or postponing them, allowing other less important but superficially more urgent or attractive activities to take their place. Given inadequate attention, tasks of this type may suddenly be promoted to the extremes of the previous category (very important and very urgent) when a deadline looms or, in the absence of any meaningful deadline, may simply not get done. Such is the fate of many life objectives that are actually very important to us but are endlessly postponed until they wither and die. Plan your time effectively to reduce this possibility, and try to ensure that as much of your time as possible is spent on tasks in this category.

Tasks that are urgent but trivial

Needless to say, you should aim to ensure that such tasks don't draw your attention away from those in the previous category. Urgency doesn't make tasks any more important. Question why they are considered urgent. Often you will find it's no more than a gloss applied by others to justify their existence or cover their own inefficiency. On the other hand, you may be the main culprit, letting something that should be a simple matter of day-to-day routine build up to a point where it becomes pressing. In such circumstances it may be necessary to give consideration to your daily work habits, so that similar situations don't arise in the future. We will give some attention to how you might do this in Chapter 3. Where an urgent but unimportant task arises from somebody else's agenda, it may be a case of challenging the other person's perception of its importance, learning to say no to requests, delegating the task or running it quietly into the sand. Of course your decision on what to do may require an element of diplomacy. If your boss is the one asking, and he or she regards a particular task as important and urgent, then some adjustment to your own assessment may be necessary.

Tasks that are neither important nor urgent

You should not be wasting your time and energy on these. Frequently, tasks in this category are used as self-generated distractions – excuses for not getting down to other more important work that for one reason or another we view with some degree of apprehension. Recognize them for what they are and focus your efforts on tasks in the other categories.

The 80:20 rule

The 80:20 rule was originated by an Italian economist – Vilfredo Pareto – around 1900. He discovered a consistent phenomenon that about 80 per cent of the wealth of countries was controlled by around 20 per cent of the people. This 80:20 principle has since been expanded to include all aspects of business and management – notably '80 per cent of the results come from 20 per cent of the effort'. The accuracy of this relationship may be disputed, but the fact remains that, by concentrating your effort into the important few actions rather than the trivial many, you are liable to achieve more impressive results.

Summary points

The first steps towards better organization consist of:

- clarifying your current organizational strengths and weaknesses;
- identifying the reasons why you are currently not as organized as you might wish;
- building a positive belief in your ability to make progress;
- establishing a clear view of what you expect to gain from better organization;
- setting precise objectives;
- balancing the different elements of your life;
- determining day-to-day priorities.

02
Organize your time

Time is unlike most other resources in that it is shared out equally. We all have the same amount of it each day. The differences between us lie in how we choose to spend it and how far we try to stretch it.

Your aim in managing your time better is either to reduce the number of hours you spend working, or to achieve more in the same number of hours. It is a matter of ordering priorities. When you say, 'I just haven't got the time for this', you are really saying, 'Something else is more important to me than this.' The problem is that, through inadequate planning and monitoring, we lose control of our schedule and fail to distinguish between the high pay-off and low pay-off demands on our time. We find ourselves saying, 'I haven't time for this' to an important commitment because we have already spent too much of it on trivia.

In this chapter, then, we will look at techniques for planning and tracking the tasks that we need to spend time on. First, however, let's consider how you currently spend your time.

How you use time now

It is helpful, before embarking on a new time-planning regime, to give attention to how you are currently spending it. Some personal organization programmes propose that you start by maintaining a rigid time log for a couple of weeks, but for those plagued by disorganization and low productivity, this may seem a wholly unreasonable starting point. I'm not going to recommend anything so demanding, but I do suggest you carry out a simple monitoring exercise for a minimum of three days.

Monitoring exercise – task importance

The purpose of this exercise is to heighten your awareness of the relative importance of the tasks which go to make up your day, and to signal those areas on which you may concentrate your efforts for improvement. On a blank sheet of paper, draw three columns and label them 'Task', 'Time' and 'Assessment'. You might also like to make a few copies, as you will be using several of these sheets in the coming days.

Keep a sheet to hand throughout your working day and note in the left hand column every activity that occupies some of your time. Give a rough estimate of the time you spend on each item in the adjacent central column. It's essential that you are honest with yourself and include everything that goes to make up your day – the important and the trivial. An accurate picture of how you are currently spending your time is vital if you are to make progress in using this limited resource more effectively. You don't need to enter much information into the 'task' column – just enough that you will remember what the item in question was.

At the end of the day, review your activity record and enter a number corresponding to the four categories of activity we encountered in the previous chapter:

1 Important and urgent.

2 Important but not urgent.

3 Urgent but not important.

4 Neither important nor urgent.

An example of how some of these entries might look is given in Figure 2.1

Figure 2.1 Monitoring task importance

Task	Time	Assessment
Attending irrelevant meeting	2 hrs	4
Planning timetable for new project	30 min	2
Responding to urgent request for information	30 min	3
Preparing for tomorrow's progress review	1 hr	1

Complete a sheet each day for a minimum of three days (preferably five) and compare them, asking yourself the following questions:

- Did I have any difficulty in distinguishing between those tasks that are important and those that are unimportant?

- If so, what steps do I need to take to remove this confusion?

- Roughly what proportion of my time is currently being spent on unimportant tasks?

- If this proportion is excessive, what could I do to reduce it?

- Was enough of my time spent on tasks which are important but not urgent?

- If the answer to the previous question is 'no', how can I increase time devoted to these tasks?

If, in the course of this exercise, you find yourself discarding or delegating tasks you would normally have carried out, that's fine. It's the start of organizing your time better.

It isn't always as easy as it might seem to distinguish between the important and the trivial, but your main reference point should be your objectives. Provided they have been well constructed, and you have taken care to break their achievement down into manageable stages, then tasks that conform to your main purposes should be quite readily identifiable. Where confusion remains, it may be necessary to re-examine and edit an objective or its constituent elements. There are, of course, different levels of importance, but I would suggest that initially you confine yourself to a simple important/trivial distinction. If you find this an inadequate means of prioritizing your time, you may wish to introduce grades of importance, but my advice would be to keep this as simple as possible (an ABC three point scale perhaps). Sometimes, despite your best efforts, a task which appears to be important subsequently turns out not to be so. Don't worry too much about this possibility. You can only make decisions based on information you have at the time.

Several of the possible strategies associated with reducing the time spent on unimportant tasks are outlined later in the book:

- Dealing with procrastination – later in this chapter.
- Maintaining concentration – Chapter 3.
- Delegating – Chapter 5.
- Overcoming distractions and interruptions – Chapter 5.
- Learning to say no – Chapter 5.

The important/urgent distinction doesn't need to be reserved solely for your professional activities. You can use it constructively in respect of your leisure time too. Many of us fritter away our free time in minor chores and distractions and discover that, as a result, our most important life-enhancing goals remain unfulfilled.

Technological applications to assist with time monitoring

If you're looking for a more technologically driven approach to monitoring your activities, you might like to consider an application such as RescueTime (www.rescuetime.com). This web-based time-management tool sits in the background and monitors your computer interactions, providing an analysis of the various applications, websites or documents you are using and offering an assessment of your productivity. If you choose to upgrade from the basic free service, it can also help you to track non-computer activity, as well as giving you the chance to voluntarily block distracting activities or to set yourself daily limits for certain types of activity and be reminded if you exceed them. Of course, what this application can't do, is make a judgement on the actual importance of the work you are undertaking. For example, you can spend an hour fiddling about on the word processor, and not producing anything of value, but RescueTime will still rate this time as very productive. So, while the application and others like it can give you an accurate reading of where your time is being spent, some input from you as to the importance and urgency of various tasks is still required.

Planning your activities

Having examined how your time is currently being spent, the next step is to adopt a workable system for planning your activities through the days, weeks and months ahead.

To plan effectively, you need first to determine your objectives and identify the steps needed to achieve them. Then it's a matter of breaking projects and assignments down into their component tasks and making an estimate of how long you expect activities to take.

This can form the basis of a master list from which you can plan your future activity. Compiling such a list is a significant undertaking and my experience suggests that it is one people often approach in a flush of enthusiasm, devoting so much time and energy to the compilation process that they are rapidly disenchanted when it comes to implementation. Seeking to incorporate too much detail in your master list at the initial stage may also result in excessive rigidity. I would suggest that it is generally better to maintain some flexibility, to review your objectives, sub-goals and tasks regularly and to be prepared to change and update them when unfolding circumstances demonstrate a need for additions or adaptations.

'To do' lists

Lists of tasks to be carried out are fundamental to most people's organizational activity, and whether a list is scribbled on the back of an envelope or flashes up on a screen, its essential purpose is the same, and so are its potential drawbacks. It can be a simple yet powerful tool or a meaningless exercise. The difference lies in how you apply it, and there are some points to bear in mind if 'to do' lists are to work for you.

As already indicated, the first question is: where does your list come from? It's not going to be a huge amount of help if it consists of just a collection of items that pop into your head each morning or at the start of each week. Such a list is likely to focus too heavily on attractive or urgent but not necessarily important issues. Drawing your immediate task schedules from a master list will certainly benefit your planning, but don't expect the master list to provide for all your needs. There are bound to be unforeseen commitments, small scale chores and requests from others that will need to be addressed.

Separate your master list into different categories to keep it manageable and in order that you can construct, view and edit particular areas of activity in isolation. Such categories may take the form of major projects or significant areas of your work. Some task-management apps come with pre-formatted categories. If you are using one of these, get rid of the irrelevant categories, and set up new ones as the need arises. I would suggest that one of your categories should be the self-development project of becoming more organized, and that it should incorporate objectives you have already identified, and others you will add as you work through this book.

Clearly, the items that make up your master list will have very different characteristics. Some will come with fixed deadlines that may incur financial or reputational penalties if not met. With others you will want to build in your own time constraints to ensure continued momentum. There is also a distinction to be made between items that can be readily completed and crossed off, and those issues you may need to focus upon for days or even weeks. Wherever possible you will have broken these down into manageable stages, but in some situations, such as when you are seeking to build a new habit, the same item may need to remain on your radar for two or three weeks until it is thoroughly embedded.

Difficulty with 'to do' lists most often occurs as a result of unrealistic expectations of the number of tasks that can be completed within a given time period. Compiling a list of tasks provides a sense of getting to grips with one's workload and it's easy to become carried away. The consequence is a list that can be daunting and may feed a tendency towards procrastination. Stress about tasks not achieved replaces the positive buzz that compiling the list provided, with a growing list of overdue items rumbling on from day to day and week to week until finally the whole exercise is abandoned.

So, in order to achieve the things you have listed it's important to keep your expectations reasonable. Setting due dates for key tasks will help you structure your progress towards the completion of projects and major objectives, but allocating dates to every task at the time you first enter them in your planner or task management app can lead to logjams, with too many tasks from different areas of activity popping up at once. Your master list will be more manageable if you get into the habit of reviewing it regularly and setting due dates for less time-critical tasks in the week or fortnight before you expect to achieve them.

Clearly, effective activity planning requires that you take account of different time frames. While the relative importance of long-term and short-term planning will vary according to the nature of your work, you may find it useful to look at planning over three time periods. The first, and most general level, might be an overall view of the next three months in terms of major objectives; the second, a week-by-week view to ensure that you are able to fit in the necessary preparation for impending commitments and deadlines; and the third, a daily plan allowing you to achieve a balance between important and urgent tasks and those that contribute towards longer term objectives.

Let's start with the most immediate.

Planning your day

The time to plan your day is not first thing in the morning, but at the end of the previous working day. Once you get into the habit it should take no more than a few minutes. The task is completed while your brain is still in work mode and the following morning you are spared indecisiveness and time-wasting. You know exactly what you are aiming to do and you are able to hit the ground running. Try not to be overambitious in the number of tasks you set yourself, and don't book yourself up so heavily that there is no space for the unexpected. You may find it helpful to divide your 'to do' lists into those tasks that are essential to achieve within the designated period and those where achievement is merely desirable. Crossing completed items off your list is very satisfying and helps to keep you on track, but resist the temptation to include too many easy hits on your list – small tasks which are there simply to be crossed off.

Mapping out your week

Just like daily planning, the time to map out your week is at the end of the previous week. You are not concerned with the same level of detail as for the daily list, but you are aiming to establish an overall balance to your week, and to ensure that you are not caught on the hop. You will be thinking about what information you need to ask for on Monday in order that it is available for a task that must be completed by Friday; what you will have to do on Tuesday to prepare for that meeting on Wednesday; how much you will need to do each day to carry forward a major long-term initiative.

A regular Friday afternoon or weekend session when you map out the coming week is also a good time to review your work in the week just passed and give yourself credit for the things you have achieved. Don't succumb to frustration about the tasks you have not managed to complete. Use the session as an opportunity to ask yourself why they haven't been completed:

- Was there over-optimism on your part with respect to the number of tasks you allocated for the week?
- Did other important and unexpected work crop up that pushed some allocated tasks aside?
- Did something occur that made the tasks no longer necessary?
- Were you perhaps guilty of procrastination or avoidance?

Consider whether the tasks concerned need to be rescheduled and, if so, slot them into your upcoming plan using, as appropriate, strategies suggested later in this chapter to ensure they are achieved. I really cannot over-emphasize the value of such review sessions.

Overviewing the next three months

This is largely about major blocks of time that will need to be devoted to projects and development tasks and is concerned with the important but non-urgent aspects of your agenda. Considerations include ensuring that:

- deadlines in respect of different assignments don't clash;
- timescales you allocate to major tasks are realistic;
- large projects or assignments are broken down into their constituent tasks;
- the order in which sub-tasks need to be completed and target completion dates are identified;
- a workable approach to monitoring progress, refining and rescheduling is in place.

If you are not currently in the habit of systematically planning your time, or your previous efforts to do so have been unsuccessful, I suggest you go for a weekly overview initially, in conjunction with a master list of 'to do' items. Once you have a system of weekly time planning up and running successfully, move on to more detailed planning of each day and an increased awareness of the longer-term dimension.

Activity tracking

Tracking is about keeping on top of the activities you have planned – ensuring that you are reminded when actions are due, and monitoring your progress towards achievement of the objectives you have set yourself. You need to retain a handle on your contacts, meetings and appointments while also maintaining clarity on what tasks are yet to be completed and when you are expecting input requested from others.

The tools you use to assist planning and tracking may range from a notebook and diary to calendar and task-management applications for smartphone or computer. My recommendation is that whatever system you use for managing personal information should be as simple as possible, consistent with the requirements of your work. Aim to get the basics right and build upon them rather than pitching in to an overly ambitious and untried system. Choose electronic applications or paper-based methods that feel comfortable and workable for you and resist the temptation to flit in and out of different methods and products. The very worst of situations is the duplication of effort and potential loss of data that can occur when your information is scattered in various locations and you have inadequate control over it.

For some people, information tracking needs may be adequately served at the simplest end of the range – a notebook to record tasks and general reminders, and a diary for appointments and timed commitments. All other tools are variations on this basic format, and increased sophistication does not always mean greater effectiveness. However, those of us with large numbers of contacts, tasks and appointments, or involvement in team activity, will want a more advanced means of tracking them. Let's look at the merits of electronic and paper-based systems.

Electronic tools

The great benefit of tracking information electronically is the way that information can be integrated and viewed in different ways, without the hassle of manually transferring it. Depending on the software you are using, you can plan your activities within a project, and slot tasks into your schedule over a period of weeks taking full account of other commitments. On the appointed date for commencement of a task, the 'to dos' will pop up and won't go away until you have signalled them as complete or rescheduled them. Regularly recurring commitments only need to be entered once. You can view the big picture and the small and link people in the address book to assignments and appointments. Routine reference information or essential notes are easily incorporated, and it is a relatively easy matter to track time and cost. You may also be able to assign tasks to others and be kept updated on progress, or to compare diaries online when seeking suitable times for a meeting. The ubiquitous smartphone means that all these actions are possible on a device you carry with you most of the time, and GPS capabilities can be harnessed to give you specific reminders when you are in a particular location.

There are numerous task and calendar applications available for devices of all sorts and aimed at users requiring varying degrees of sophistication. Many are free of charge at the basic level but may have the option of a paid account to unlock more sophisticated features or access for multiple users. At the simple end of the range are products such as Microsoft To Do, Google Tasks and Apple Reminders, and even at the basic level it is possible to introduce some degree of sophistication, for example by allocating sub-tasks or delegating responsibility for completion.

Where your work involves complex project activity or significant teamwork, more overtly collaborative software may be called for. Once again, there are plenty of suitable candidates. Two popular products at the time of writing are Monday.com and ClickUp, but there are many other widely used and well-regarded examples.

Some applications, such as the full version of Outlook (Microsoft 365), bundle all aspects of personal information management – email, contacts, calendar and task lists – in one integrated package, while other options require the employment of two or three applications to get the full range of tools. Integration is clearly desirable, but a combination of separate tools may offer capabilities not present in a single application.

In an environment where many of us now use multiple electronic devices, a primary consideration has to be the synchronization of data between them. This is rendered more straightforward if you are using the same operating system and applications on all your devices, but increasingly developers are releasing products that operate on different platforms and synchronize data between rival applications. If you're currently using old software and are encountering synchronization issues, it may be worth checking to see whether there is an update that will solve your problems.

Should you find yourself in the unfortunate position of being unable to sync data between devices, then at least make sure you have one master device and rigorously ensure you keep it up to date. Your phone is the most obvious candidate for this role as it's something you carry with you at most times and is consequently on hand for entering new commitments and receiving reminders about existing ones.

Ultimately, the choice of which electronic applications to use is down to personal preference, and there are scores of similarly competent products both free and paid for. New products and updates are appearing all the time, so an internet search along the lines of 'best time management apps' may help with recommendations.

Paper-based planners and organizers

Electronic handling of organizational data isn't for everyone. In the days before smartphones and Wi-Fi, no self-respecting professional would be seen without a leather-bound personal organizer, and a visit to an office stationery supplier today will reveal that there are still plenty around, produced in a variety of styles and prices. The basic format is a small ring binder with indexed sections containing pre-printed insert pages. Typical inserts available include: year planners; diaries in various formats; daily planning sheets; monthly objectives and project planning sheets; telephone and address book inserts; budget and expenses planning sheets; and pages for notes.

The idea is that all necessary working information is contained in one convenient folder. Users can switch their attention easily from a long-term to a short-term view and can swiftly update information wherever they might be. New pages can be inserted and redundant ones removed so that the organizer remains indefinitely expandable and always up to date. The downside is that there may be some need to transfer information from one page to another and some of the tools, year planners for example, are a little too small for serious use. Also, if you have a large number of contacts for your address book or need to make a lot of notes, you can find these sections becoming unwieldy.

What is best – electronic or paper?

It all depends on how you like to work. Paper-based systems are clearly much less powerful in terms of cross-referencing, and require a degree of duplication. They lack the facility for automatic reminders and it's easier for items to get lost. On the other hand, even allowing for the voice-generated methods available on modern devices, inputting or extracting information from electronic systems can interrupt the flow of other activities.

There is no doubt that we are increasingly turning to technology to assist our personal organization, but it is not yet time to declare an end to paper-based methods. Even the most technologically committed of us will admit to tasks where we prefer to use paper – for example, when mapping out the activities to be included within a project before getting down to detailed planning. And there are well regarded practitioners in the time-management business who strongly advocate managing tasks by paper-based means.

It is very important that whatever means you choose to initially log commitments and things to do should be accessible at all times. Your brain will often alert you to something you need to do when you are engaged in an entirely unrelated activity. By recording it immediately you are freed up to concentrate fully on the task that is currently occupying you.

For my part, whilst I use electronic apps extensively for appointments and major tasks, I will always keep a notebook to hand, often preferring to make a scribbled note to be entered later rather than interrupt the flow of other activities in order to interact with an electronic device. Minor tasks frequently get done while still in the notebook.

Activity

Before leaving this section, take a few moments to consider how you currently plan and track your activity, the weaknesses that are apparent and the changes you might make.
How do you currently plan your activity?

1 Long-term task plan.

2 Weekly schedule.

3 Daily 'to do' list.
4 Other.

What weaknesses are apparent in your current approach?

1 Lists completed but then ignored.

2 Attractive tasks completed first; unattractive ones postponed.

3 Bottlenecks with too many tasks scheduled within a given period.

4 Information stored in different locations.

5 Inadequate review of progress.
6 Other.

What changes do you intend to make that will aim to address present planning and tracking weaknesses? Enter these in your master list and work on them in due course.

Scheduling your time – estimating time requirements

You start the day with, let's say, a dozen items that you hope to complete from your 'to do' list. What confidence do you have that at the end of the day they will all have been crossed off? Not a great deal unless you have made some estimate of how long each task is likely to take, and fitted them in with the other commitments that make up your day. It isn't just about the confidence and credibility boost that comes from achieving what you set out to do, although that should not be underestimated. Estimating time requirements of tasks allows you to use the available slots in your day appropriately. If you have half an hour between commitments, you want, wherever possible, to fill it with a half-hour task. Discovering that a task you thought was going to take half an hour is really going to take an hour may result in additional time spent refocusing your attention when you eventually come back to it.

You will never achieve time estimation perfection. Tasks will contain unforeseen elements, and we all have a tendency to overestimate the time taken to complete those tasks we dislike, and to underestimate the ones we like. But taking a moment to think about what is involved with a task before you pop it into your schedule can greatly help the management of your working day.

Slotting tasks into the day

Your day is likely to be made up of fixed commitments – appointments and regular scheduled elements – and flexible ones – the tasks on your 'to do' list. Having roughly estimated the time you expect these tasks to take, you can then get an idea of when you will hope to fit them in. Don't seek to rigidly plan your whole day in advance, and don't spend a lot of time on the process. It should be a quick and simple way of giving your day shape and balance, fitting tasks into appropriate time slots, not a bureaucratic exercise. Half-hour time slots are a manageable way of dividing up your day, although for some smaller tasks you may want to think in terms of quarter-hour slots. Group several minor tasks – five or six phone calls for example – into a half-hour slot. Allow a bit of padding in your time estimates for some of the inevitable calls and interruptions. There is a great satisfaction boost to be had from completing a task in less than the time you expected it to take, but you also need to maintain your cool when tasks are taking longer than planned. Above all, stay flexible and deal with whatever the day throws at you.

Activity – improving your scheduling accuracy

If it isn't your current practice to estimate the time that tasks will occupy, start by setting a rough estimate alongside each item in your 'to do' list. Once you are under way, monitor the accuracy of your time planning for several days:

- Give a rough time estimate to every task on your daily 'to do' list.
- When you complete the task, enter the actual time taken alongside the estimate.
- Compare the differences over the period of a week.
- Are there any patterns of consistent over- or underestimation?
- Are there reasons you can discern for the inaccuracy?
- What can you do to improve accuracy?

Procrastination

Some element of postponement is both inevitable and necessary in a busy life, but we give ourselves needless stress and may greatly reduce our effectiveness if we engage in habitual procrastination. It's one of the biggest time-management problems for many of us, and we need to take a look at why it occurs and what we can do about it.

The first thing to make clear is that procrastination isn't just about laziness or lack of resolve. If you view the habit as one which can be dealt with simply by showing greater determination, then you may well be disappointed. Many procrastinators find that resolutions to change their ways may work for a while, but then the bad habits start to recur. To achieve a more lasting response to procrastination we need first to understand the reasons for it. These may be complex and varied, and I have only the space here to give a brief outline of the possible causes, but let's look at some of the major reasons, starting with the most straightforward.

Dislike of particular tasks

Most of us have tasks that we would prefer not to be landed with. Whether it's general office housekeeping, keeping our finances up to date or responding to routine emails, we tend to postpone those we perceive as boring or bureaucratic until they have built up to the point that they cannot be ignored. By this stage completion may have turned into a major exercise, and this only serves to re-inforce the sense of dislike, and to ensure that similar tasks will be the subject of further procrastination in the future.

Capacity for distraction

The ability to concentrate on the task in hand without resorting to self-generated diversions is an increasingly rare skill in our modern world. We know what we should be spending our time on, and we may even be relishing getting our teeth into it, and yet we experience a curious resistance. We seize upon any excuse to direct our attention elsewhere – checking email inboxes, texting friends, engaging in aimless browsing or doing a bit of social networking. We tell ourselves, 'It will only take a couple of minutes to do this', but once the interruption occurs it leads on to other distraction activity, and half an hour is frittered away in the blink of an eye.

In our modern environment, characterized as it is by an over-abundance of information, multiplicity of choices and immediacy of electronic communication, routes to distraction are much more prevalent than they used to be. The incidence of procrastination appears to be rising as a consequence. In a study carried out by the University of Calgary, it has been noted that the average self-assessment score for tendency towards procrastination has risen by 39 per cent in the past 25 years. The author of the study Professor Piers Steel says, 'It's never been harder to be self-disciplined in all of history than it is now.'

Desire not to offend

When faced with requests from others, most of us make an effort to be polite and helpful, even when the request concerns a task we would prefer not to have, or may not even be equipped to perform. A common and quite understandable response is to agree to the request but then to postpone execution, resulting in additional stress for the person accepting the task and frustration for the individual making the request. In such circumstances, it may be far better to take an assertive line, and say no to the request at the outset. We will examine how you might do this in Chapter 5.

Overly optimistic time assessments

Failure to gauge accurately the amount of time or work required to complete a task is a common problem that often accompanies a task we may be resisting for other reasons. A consequence is that we postpone commencement to such a point that the job cannot be fulfilled on time or its completion is rushed and inadequate.

Fear of failure

This is possibly the most prevalent reason for procrastination and the one least likely to be acknowledged. Many outwardly successful and confident people are plagued by a deep-seated fear of failure or of appearing foolish in the eyes of others. This is most generally the result of past experiences, and possibly insecurities generated in childhood. The anxiety about failing leads to a variety of responses:

- Catastrophizing – predicting the worst possible outcome from any proposed course of action, and allowing it to become a reason for inaction.

- Pretending to ourselves – inventing good reasons why the feared activity should not be carried out.

- Using other tasks as distractions or shields to prevent us having to face up to those that make us anxious.

- Setting hugely ambitious targets that have no realistic prospect of achievement, but where the perceived stigma of failure is much lower than it would be for a more modest target. If the individual fails, then he or she is able to take comfort in the knowledge that the target was close to impossible from the outset.

For those of us who fear failure, inaction can feel like a safer option than the anticipated pain of not succeeding. But the more we avoid those things that make us anxious, the greater the fear becomes. Initial avoidance eases our anxiety, and that leads us to employ the same strategy next time a similar situation presents itself. And by avoiding the things that make us anxious we give ourselves no opportunity to test the validity of our fears, so the exaggerations and distortions are reinforced. With each incidence of avoidance it becomes more difficult to face up to whatever we are afraid of. The difficult phone call, the confrontational meeting or the tough project that we have repeatedly postponed and worried about becomes almost impossible to contemplate. We are locked into a vicious spiral of avoidance.

Perfectionism

You might be surprised to see perfectionism in a list of reasons for procrastination. Surely a perfectionist is going to take pains to ensure that tasks are completed in a timely and effective manner. Undoubtedly, there are successful perfectionists for whom this is the case, but for many the opposite is true. People with a tendency towards perfectionism frequently place unrealistic demands upon themselves. They set the bar very high and then procrastinate over achievement of tasks. There is an underlying sense that if the high standards set are not achieved, the individual will be deemed less worthwhile as a person. Procrastination therefore becomes a tool to avoid unpleasant confrontations with reality. Where a task is postponed to the point that completion has to be rushed and imperfect, the individual is able to avoid uncomfortable judgements with excuses such as, 'I could have done much better if only I had started sooner.'

These are just some of the reasons why people procrastinate. If you are someone whose personal organization is hampered by this habit, and many of us are, you need to give some attention to why it occurs in your own case. As with most problems, recognition of its existence is the first step to overcoming it. Keep an eye on any tendency to feed yourself excuses. Observe yourself over the coming days and look for any signs of resistance to particular tasks. Ask yourself what the reasons are – fear and anxiety, boredom, distractibility, perfectionism – the same ones will not always apply. Once you have identified the reason(s) it's easier to select the most appropriate strategies for overcoming the problem.

Strategies for beating procrastination

Once again I'm restricted in the amount of space I can devote to tackling this problem, but what follows aims to be a concise set of 10 approaches that you may find useful in tackling this most stubborn of habits.

1. Don't fear fear

Recognize that it's OK to be anxious. Fears are made worse for many of us because we fear the very sensation of fear. We don't want to put ourselves in situations where we will encounter that sense of apprehension and discomfort, and so we stick doggedly to those things that we know will not put us in danger of it. But the experiences that make us afraid may also have the potential to offer us the greatest amounts of achievement and fulfilment, and the apprehension we feel before embarking upon them should be part of gearing ourselves up to give of our best. Most entertainers and sports people will testify to the fact that a certain degree of fear is a prerequisite to a really great performance. It's a matter of proportional response – a level of apprehension that brings out the best we have to offer and does not tip us into avoidance and paralysis.

Recognize too that you are the one who created these fears and anxieties, and that they don't exist anywhere other than inside your head. So, take ownership of them and acknowledge that what you have made you can overcome. Once you have achieved this attitude shift it is harder to invent excuses or to see your anxieties as insurmountable blocks placed in your way. Standing up to them becomes a matter of motivation rather than ability.

2. Get the pain balance right

The prospect of carrying out the tasks you are avoiding involves an element of anticipated pain, but not doing them involves actual pain. The problem is that while the anticipated pain is envisaged as a big hit – one that gets worse the longer a task is postponed – the actual pain of not carrying out the task comes in the form of a steady low-level irritation. You need to adjust the balance between the two, so that the pain of not doing the task outweighs the anticipated pain of doing it. You can achieve this by: clarifying in your own mind the consequences of procrastination in terms of loss of control over your life, introducing penalties for non-performance, making a public commitment or opening yourself to be held to account for completion of certain tasks. Tackle anticipated pain by noting the frequency with which tasks you have been avoiding turn out less fearsome than expected. Use this knowledge as a reference to help overcome future anxieties.

Similarly, address the pleasure side of the equation. What pleasure do you get from procrastination? The answer, generally, is none. How will you feel if you fulfil the tasks you are currently resisting? Focus on the end of a week in which you have achieved everything you set out to do, and visualize what completion will feel like.

3. Give yourself positive messages

The tendency to feed ourselves negative messages is most acute with those things that make us anxious or afraid. The prospect of tackling your fears becomes overwhelming if you are simultaneously filling your head with statements such as: 'I'm never going to manage this.' 'It's too scary.' 'Might as well give up now.' It's most important to approach feared activities in a positive frame of mind. If you think you can't do it then you can't. But just as negative self-talk diminishes your ability to act, positive affirmations can boost it. Choose some upbeat and constructive statements and mentally rehearse them at times you need to strengthen your resolve.

4. Use visualization

Visualization allows you to rehearse a situation liable to generate anxiety in a relaxed and controlled manner before the event. It's a technique best known in the sports arena, but can apply equally to other forms of human endeavour. Routinely picturing yourself succeeding at upcoming challenges serves to remove psychological limitations you may have placed on yourself, and it has been shown that during the mental rehearsal of visualization, two-thirds of the brain activity is the same as when the activity is carried out for real. We are enabled to approach an activity we have visualized with an attitude closely resembling that which comes from successful previous experience.

Let's look at a typical example of a situation in which visualization might assist – a tricky meeting with a forceful individual in which you have to make a complaint, justify your actions or administer a reprimand. Before you start, make sure that you are fully relaxed and untroubled by distractions or extraneous thoughts. If you have previous less than satisfactory experience of a similar situation, you may like to introduce some soothing triggers into your visualization – a favourite piece of relaxing music perhaps, or some calming deep breathing. As you run the visualization, you mentally rehearse all aspects of the interview – your confident body language, eye contact, tone of voice, the sorts of words you use. Picture yourself handling the situation successfully and assertively, but don't ignore the anxiety that would be a normal accompaniment to such a meeting. Sense it, but visualize yourself overcoming it – remaining relaxed and in control – and recognize the strong sense of self-worth that comes with your assured performance.

Remember that visualization is a supplement to, not a replacement for, other preparation, and it's not a means of achieving things that are simply beyond your skill level. If possible, run a visualization several times to make a real difference, taking account of the different responses, including negative ones, that you might receive from the other person. Remember that you can only control your behaviour, not that of the other party, and take care not to over-rehearse to the point that you become less agile in dealing with any unexpected responses. If any negative elements come into the picture, gently move them away, without allowing anger and frustration to develop.

5. Reverse the order

Don't allow postponed tasks to build up a head of steam to the point where they become even more difficult to tackle. Arrange your list of things to do with the least appealing tasks at the top of the list and the ones you enjoy most at the bottom. Tackle the list in order and, not only do you get the relief that comes from overcoming challenges that otherwise might be postponed, but you are also rewarded with successively more attractive tasks as you work your way down the list.

6. Make firm commitments

As mentioned in the section on objectives, you should always ensure that what you set out to do is achievable. Anything that makes it onto your 'to do' list should be a firm commitment and not just a vague intention. Keep the list short to start with, and review what you have achieved at the end of every day and every week.

When you have resolved to tackle something you might be inclined to postpone, get on with it as soon as possible. The longer you leave it, the more you will find yourself inventing excuses for non-completion. Where the activity is not one you can deal with immediately, at least do something that commits you – arrange an appointment or schedule a time when you will deal with it.

7. Schedule tasks

Tasks that you don't like or are resisting demand a lot of mental energy just getting to the point where you're ready to tackle them. Often this is way out of proportion to their importance. You can greatly reduce this if you take action to ritualize tedious recurring tasks by including them at set times in your schedule until they become embedded routines that demand little mental energy. We will look at mobilizing the power of habit a little more fully in the next chapter.

8. Take controlled breaks

Tackle boredom and loss of focus by allowing yourself short controlled breaks at pre-determined times, or when a certain proportion of a task has been completed, but maintain your discipline to ensure the breaks don't become a distraction from the main task. If you need some help with this, there are various applications for phone and computer that can be set to remind you when to take a break and when to get back to work. A couple of these are mentioned in the 'useful tools' section of Chapter 8. For other examples, try entering words such as 'break reminder' into an internet search engine.

9. Record successes

It is very important to hang on to the sense of accomplishment that follows from successfully dealing with a task you have been resisting. Remember how different it feels from the temporary relief of avoidance. Note also how situations seldom turn out to be as difficult as you had feared. Keeping a diary may seem like a mundane activity, but it's a hugely valuable means of charting a way through difficult issues, reviewing progress and giving yourself positive reinforcement for a job well done. It can also be a valuable resource to draw upon if similar problems recur.

10. Make it easier

Rather than working through all tasks in a linear fashion, look for an easy point of entry to those where you have been unsure how to get started. The important thing is to make a start at whatever point.

Short bursts of concentrated activity – from five minutes to an hour – can work well as a way of overcoming inertia. They serve to overcome the psychological obstacle posed by a difficult or daunting task. You can amaze yourself by how much it is possible to achieve in just a few minutes and, if you punch holes in a task by this means, suddenly the task is no longer daunting and you are starting to achieve the momentum needed to carry you towards completion.

Similarly, divide large and complicated tasks into bite sized chunks so that they appear less formidable.

Activity – ask yourself

1 What are the types of task over which I'm inclined to procrastinate? (List them)

2 Which of the identified reasons for procrastination apply in my case?

- Dislike of particular tasks.

- Capacity for distraction.

- Desire not to offend.

- Overly optimistic time assessments.

- Fear of failure.

- Perfectionism.

- Other.

3 Which of the ten strategies for tackling procrastination could I usefully apply?

- Dealing with fear and anxiety.

- Achieving appropriate pain balance.

- Producing positive statements.

- Visualization.

- Reversing the order.

- Making firm commitments.

- Ritualizing recurring tasks.

- Scheduling breaks.

- Recording successes.

- Generating momentum.

Formulate objectives where appropriate, and enter them in the 'organize yourself' section of your master list.

Meeting deadlines

There are five main reasons why deadlines aren't met:

- The deadline is unrealistic to start with.

- The deadline is inadequately planned for.

- The person responsible for meeting the deadline is unable to get started on the task.

- The person responsible for meeting the deadline is let down by others.

- The person responsible for meeting the deadline spends more time on the assignment than necessary.

Dealing with unrealistic deadlines

The best time to counteract an unrealistic deadline is when it is being set. If you think that you are being asked to work to a deadline that isn't feasible, show that you have thought through the timescale rather than simply rejecting the proposal out of hand. Adopt a positive problem-solving attitude. Set out the stages that will need to be met in order to deliver on time, and explore whether there are any ways through the difficulty – such as additional resources which would help you to meet the required timescale – or whether it is possible for the deadline to be reconsidered. Unfortunately, deadlines are seldom set in a perfect working world, and while the timescale for a project may seem reasonable when viewed in isolation, the chances are that it will cut across other assignments that also have deadlines. One tactic you can adopt with the person setting the deadline is to ask them whether it takes priority over the other deadlines you are working to, and if so, which they would wish you to set back in order to meet the timescale on the new job. Remember too that some of the least realistic deadlines are the ones we set ourselves. Just as we pile too many activities into our daily 'to do' lists, so we overestimate just what we will be able to achieve in the coming weeks and months.

In some circumstances there may be deadlines that are unrealistic but not subject to influence. They may arise from the requirements of external bodies, regulators or clients. If affected, the only solution is to address the other demands on your time to free the space that will allow the deadline to be met. Once again, it is essential that you do this early enough to make a difference.

Before you start work, make sure you are completely clear what is required of you, what resources you have at your disposal, and what additional support you may call upon if necessary. Failure to deal with these issues is a frequent cause of missed deadlines.

Planning to meet your deadline

OK, so you have accepted the deadline. You now need to plan your implementation of it. Break the assignment or project down into a series of stages which will lead you to a successful conclusion and try to estimate the amount of time each will take. Calculate the number of working days between now and the planned completion date and ask yourself what you will need to do each week (or each day if you are dealing with a short deadline) in order to achieve it. Build in sufficient slack to allow for unexpected events and delays, and make sure that, in estimating the time needed for each stage, you have taken account of the other commitments which have a call on your time.

As you work towards completion of your project, use the finishing point for each of the stages as a milestone – a point at which you can monitor your progress, and ensure that you are on track. Use them also to give yourself the positive reinforcement necessary to maintain motivation. If you are able to get ahead of your schedule at any time, resist the temptation to slacken off. Use the time to build in some additional flexibility at the end of the project. The tidying up elements are often the ones most likely to be underestimated.

Inability to get down to work

This tendency frequently accompanies poor planning. It may be that you are not sure you have all the information you need in order to make a start or just that the finish date seems such a long way off. You convince yourself that you have ample time and will be sure to get down to it in a day or two. People will often procrastinate over the start of a project because they lack confidence in their ability to succeed at it, or they are unsure where to start. If affected by this, then cast aside worries about tackling the task at the beginning, and simply pitch in at whatever point appears to be the most straightforward. The momentum you gain from making inroads into the task will usually outweigh any inefficiencies resulting from stages tackled out of order.

Avoid being let down by others

Often, completion of a project or assignment will not be entirely in your hands, and you will be reliant on input from others if you are to meet your deadline. Once again good planning is the key to ensuring that others don't present problems for you. Recognize that they will have priorities of their own, which are likely to differ from yours. Let them know in plenty of time what it is you require from them and the date by which you will need their input. It generally helps to set this date a few days before you actually need it so that any laxity on their part doesn't throw out the schedule for any subsequent work you need to do with their input. Make your requirements as clear as possible so as to avoid any misinterpretation.

Don't go over the top in seeking perfection

This is often a trait that signals lack of confidence. It may be a matter of research or information gathering which is out of proportion with the task in hand and results in the person undertaking the task becoming bogged down and unable to see the wood for the trees. Or it may be unwillingness to let go of the project – relentlessly honing and polishing it with the aim of producing the perfect job. You need to avoid both these tendencies and recognize the point at which further effort does not produce a commensurate return.

Activity – ask yourself

- What difficult deadlines have I been faced with recently?
- What were the reasons for the difficulty?
- How do I need to change my way of working in order to address such problems in future?

Devise objectives as appropriate and enter on your master 'to do' list.

Summary points

If you are to organize your time more effectively, you need to:

- be aware of the way your time is currently spent;
- be able to plan your activity over different time frames;
- select tracking tools that work for you;
- estimate the time required to complete tasks;
- work to reduce procrastination;
- adopt an organized approach to meeting deadlines.

03
Understand the way you work

After planning and prioritizing your work and taking steps to manage your time, the next point to consider is the way in which you set about it. In this chapter, we shall examine four features of your approach to tasks which can greatly improve effectiveness: scheduling tasks at appropriate times; working in short bursts to maintain concentration; mobilizing the power of habit; and dealing with decisions systematically.

Schedule tasks at appropriate times

It is likely that your workload consists of a variety of different tasks. You will have limited jurisdiction over when to carry out those that are dependent on the availability of others, but for the majority of tasks there will be some flexibility on timing. Most tasks will fall into one of three broad groups:

- *maintenance tasks* – those routine jobs which are essential to keep you functioning properly, staying informed, dealing with the normal inflow and outflow of information, organizing your workspace, completing routine correspondence;

- *people tasks* – negotiating, participating in meetings, persuading, reviewing performance, networking, resolving problems or complaints, presenting, training, interviewing;

- *creative, planning and problem-solving tasks* – preparing plans and project briefs, writing reports, analysing information and drawing conclusions, finding solutions to problems, generating new ideas.

These are just a few examples. Depending on the nature of your job, there will be others appropriate to you.

Recognize the demands that different tasks place on you

Generally speaking, the maintenance tasks will make the most limited energy demands. Later in this chapter we will look at how many of them can be made even less demanding by harnessing the power of habit. Creative, planning and problem-solving tasks will normally require the greatest amount of concentrated attention and also larger blocks of time because of the need to get yourself up to speed before you are able to make significant progress. People tasks may be of long or short duration, but are frequently the ones which make the greatest demands on emotional energy. Those that may involve an element of confrontation are particularly draining. If you have several of these tasks, try tackling them together – one after the other. The head of steam you build up to tackle the first helps to carry you through the subsequent ones and, overall, you will find it less emotionally draining than having to gear yourself up for each one individually.

We are all familiar with the idea of a body clock which regulates our sleeping and waking. Anybody who has ever worked a night shift or crossed time zones will testify to the havoc caused by its disruption. But we give much less attention to the peaks and troughs of alertness that occur throughout our waking lives, and which vary significantly between individuals. Needless to say, the alertness cycles in your day can have a potent effect on performance and it pays to schedule your most demanding tasks at the times you are best able to deal with them.

What are your best times?

We are accustomed to describing ourselves in general terms – 'I'm a morning person', 'I do my best work in the evening' – but have you ever looked at your work patterns in more than the most cursory terms? You may have become locked into a way of working not particularly suited to your body rhythms as a result of difficulties in organizing your day. You may assume, for example, that evenings are the times when you do your best planning and problem-solving activity, when in fact those tasks have been squeezed into that end of the day because you have found it impossible to give them the concentrated thought they require amid the distractions and interruptions of normal working hours. If, as a result of better organization, you are able to deal more effectively with interruptions, you may find that you can readdress your assumptions about the best times to take on particular tasks.

I suggest that you start by engaging in a little experimentation over the course of a week or two. Try moving tasks from when you might habitually do them and assess the results on your output. For example, many of us start our working day by checking and responding to emails and, given the volume of such correspondence routinely found in many workplaces, this task can occupy a significant chunk of the working day. However, email is often a low-demand maintenance task and dealing with one's inbox frequently offers only limited progress on the things that matter. Using possible high-energy times at the start of your working day to tackle more demanding tasks and leaving email until later (possibly just before lunch) may result in improvements to both the quality of your work and your output.

If there are people or problem-solving tasks liable to weigh upon your mind and distract you from other activities in the course of the day, then try slotting them in early on so that you will be free of their distracting influence.

In today's pressured working environment, many of us have become night owls – choosing to knock off a task or two shortly before going to bed. If this is your habit, and I'm afraid it has

Table 3.1 Time-shifting tasks

Task	Usual time (am/pm)	New time (am/pm)	Conclusions
1			
2			
3			
4			
5			

often been mine over the years, then at least ensure that such tasks are not the sort that require you to sit in front of a computer screen or will leave you mentally overstimulated. Both have been proven disruptive to good-quality sleep, which has an undoubted impact on your productivity the following day.

Don't just look at morning and evening peaks and troughs, but consider whether there are energy peaks that might be exploited at other times of the day – early afternoon for example.

After experimenting for a couple of weeks, assess the outcomes to see whether there is any pattern of activity that warrants change. Make adjustments to your schedule and note any improvements in performance.

A simple template such as the one in Table 3.1 may help you assess the benefits of some task time-shifting.

Why you can't always rely on the same body rhythms

Your normal pattern of energy peaks is a good guide to the times when you should schedule your most demanding tasks, but don't regard it as infallible. On the days when you are slightly under the weather, or at the end of an exhausting week, there may be no appreciable energy peaks and any sort of demanding activity is a struggle. If you have any choice in the matter, don't labour on with a difficult task that is not working for you. In these circumstances you are unlikely to break through into sunny pastures. Far better to switch to a more routine maintenance task and return to the intensive one when you are rested and re-energized. Beware, however, of using this as simply an excuse for procrastination.

On the reverse side of the coin, when things are going particularly well, don't stop just because you have reached today's target. If you have energy and creativity to spare, and a task is flowing for you – go with it. Keep your schedules flexible and be prepared to listen to your body.

Fit the task to your available time

There are some tasks that you can only set about if you have a significant chunk of time – you need to gather resources around you, get yourself into the right frame of mind and make sure that you are free of interruptions. Other tasks you can dip in and out of more quickly. Don't waste your time trying to gear up for a long-slot task when you only have a short slot available. Retain some quick payoff tasks, such as small but essential administrative chores or necessary responses to routine messages, for those spare moments when somebody due for an appointment is running late, when a meeting doesn't start on time, or while you are waiting for a train.

Maintain concentration and motivation

Our capacity for sustained concentration will vary according to the nature of the task, the time of day and the degree of distraction, but even at the best of times it is finite. When tackling lengthy, mentally intensive tasks we need both milestones and breaks that allow us to maintain our focus. But as we have already noted, it's easy to slip into disorganized habits, whereby breaks become diversions that take on a momentum of their own. Successfully negotiate your way through lengthy tasks by adopting the following rules:

1 Examine the task in hand. What are you aiming to achieve and to what standard? What is the timescale for the overall task, and how might you break it down into smaller elements? Even if you are under significant time pressure, it's generally worth spending a little time addressing these points. When you get to work on the task, it will be with greater clarity and sense of purpose.

2 Set yourself a succession of clear, timed targets, each with an element of challenge that is demanding but achievable. One popular approach holds that a period of 25-minutes activity followed by a 5-minute break offers the best formula for maintenance of concentration and motivation, but I would suggest that you vary timings according to the task and your own energy levels. A period of between 30 and 60 minutes for each target is generally the most workable. You may be able to concentrate on some tasks for a longer period, but unless you have achieved the unforced but highly productive state known as 'flow', attention is likely to be on the wane after this time. A tough challenge to be achieved in an hour is less daunting than one that you expect to take two, and you're also less likely to cut yourself any slack. It's possible to blast away at a task for this length of time and achieve more than you thought possible.

3 The timed element to your target is important for a disciplined approach to the job, but go for the achievement of your target task rather than sticking rigidly to the time allocation. If you achieve it in less than the target time, so much the better – give yourself a pat on the back. If it takes a little longer than you thought, then stick with it to completion. Only if a task element is taking a lot longer than anticipated or you hit a complete brick wall should you reassess your expectations. In such a situation you might set a lesser target to be achieved within the chosen time period, or look for a way of getting past the obstacle

that has blocked your progress – perhaps seeking a different angle on the problem or moving to a new part of the overall task with a view to returning to the problematic area later. Don't permit an unexpected hitch to be an excuse for downing tools.

4 At the end of each target period, before you take a break, set your next target task and consider how you aim to tackle it. That way, you will be returning to work in progress, and the effort of refocusing will be significantly less.

5 OK, you can take that break now. Just a few minutes doing something different is generally enough. It might be an opportunity to stretch your legs or relax your eyes after a sustained spell of computer activity, a quick and easy maintenance task or an undemanding phone call. What matters is that it should be different from the other activity you have been engaged in, and you should not allow it to develop into a lengthy diversion. If supplementary issues arise, give them their own entries on your 'to do' list and get back to the main activity.

Mobilize the power of habit

You only have a finite amount of energy each day and you want to be able to expend it as productively as possible. But the chances are that all sorts of trivial and time-wasting tasks are using up your available resources and preventing you pushing forward those larger projects which require sustained concentration and effort. By enlisting the power of habit, you can free up the energy you need to devote to the intensive tasks which will really make a difference to your effectiveness. If you pride yourself in bringing an element of creativity to your work and have an instinctive antipathy towards anything that smacks of becoming a creature of habit, console yourself in the knowledge that having some habits and routines in your day can give you more energy to tackle the creative things at other times. Routines are also valuable for dealing with boring tasks that you might be inclined to postpone.

Consider the routines you go through when you get up in the morning – cleaning your teeth for example. They have become ingrained – part of the way you start your day. Your thoughts are elsewhere while you are doing them – listening to the radio or planning your day – and you don't worry about them. They demand no mental energy. There are tasks in your working day which can be turned into the equivalent of cleaning your teeth. They may not permit quite the same level of mental detachment, but they're tasks which currently use up unnecessary energy. They vie with all the other demands upon you for a place on your busy schedule – you have to decide when to do them, and worry about them when they are not done.

A number of the general organizational tasks featured in this book may usefully be made the subject of habits and routines. They include:

- updating your schedules for the following day/week – Chapter 2;
- handling incoming information – Chapter 4;
- keeping your workspace clear and organized – Chapter 6;
- carrying out routine filing and computer housekeeping – Chapter 7.

There will be others specific to your job. On the flip side of positive habits which can free up our energies for more important activity are current negative work habits which condemn us to ineffectiveness.

CASE STUDY

Frances Craig is a classic example of someone whose work habits limit effectiveness. She works amid overwhelming and distracting clutter of both physical and virtual varieties. Not only is there time wasted looking for things among the disorganized heaps of material around her office, but her habit of failing to deal with emails effectively, and of trying to multitask several activities at once, means that similar problems affect her computer-based work. She is conscious that with more discipline she could work a deal more effectively, and engages in periodic purges of printed material and email backlogs, during which important communications are liable to get ditched with the junk, but so far she has not succeeded in building up regular habits that will allow her to locate information speedily and focus on one issue at a time.

What fixes habits?

Habits, positive or negative, are fixed by repetition and reinforcement. Everybody is aware of the role that repetition plays in habit formation, but often we fail to persist for long enough to make a new routine automatic. We need to remember also that repetition will only work if it is accompanied by reinforcement.

Reinforcement can be positive or negative. Often overlooked examples of positive reinforcement include a word of congratulation (even if it comes from yourself) or simply the boost that comes from crossing an item off your 'to do' list. Negative reinforcement may come in the form of unwelcome discomfort. Some reinforcers are stronger than others. Those that are clear and immediate tend to have more effect than those that are vague and in the future. In the case of Frances and her work habits, the consequences of any different way of behaving are vague and indefinite by comparison with the immediate reinforcement provided by her current work habit, which she perceives as the ability to move quickly and easily from one job to another with the minimum of preparation or clear-up time. To change her behaviour she needs to make a deliberate connection between different habits and their consequences, and to work on reinforcing them every time she exhibits the desired behaviour.

Habits are also bolstered by your environment – including your own attitudes and perceptions of self, those close to you and the prevailing culture in your place of work. Frances's view of herself as a busy, creative type is a part of the background to her behaviour, as is the tendency in her organization to view multitasking as a characteristic to be applauded.

It follows from all this that simply deciding you are going to introduce new routines into your working day is no guarantee of success. You need to address the environment in which your current behaviour flourishes, and work on nurturing and reinforcing the desired habits until they become automatic. It won't happen immediately but the end result will be worth a bit of persistence.

Activity – ask yourself

- Which of my current work habits contribute to effective performance?
- What are the work habits that limit effective performance?
- What new habits could I develop to improve performance?

If you find this task difficult, it may help to observe your work habits for a few days and return to it.

Tips for changing habits

1 Start thinking in positive terms about the habit you are working to develop. Associate it with desirable outcomes – the chance to free up time and energy for creative and enjoyable jobs – rather than focusing on the boring and mundane nature of the task itself.

2 Similarly, associate new habits with positive aspects of your self-image. They are essential parts of your creativity and decisiveness rather than routines that bring out your bureaucratic traits.

3 Change the environment in which those habits you wish to change currently flourish. For example, coincide a change in desk organization with an overall purge on your workspace.

4 Seek to replace bad work habits with others that have beneficial impact. For example, if workplace stress leads you to flit into wasteful distraction activities such as social media or aimless web browsing, try alternatives that directly bear on the source of the problem. A few minutes spent on relaxation or breathing exercises, mindfulness or simply getting away from your computer and moving around, may allow you to return to your main task with renewed focus and energy.

5 Remember that immediate positive reinforcement is what fixes new habits. This might come in the form of crossing an item off your 'to do' list, rewarding yourself with a desirable outcome (now I can go home, now I can go to lunch) or simply congratulating yourself on a task completed. Give yourself immediate positive reinforcement every time you engage in the new behaviour.

6 Hang any new routines onto key times in your working day. First thing, just before lunch, immediately after lunch, just before you go home. Associating them with constant landmarks makes them less likely to be overlooked.

7 Continue reinforcing and monitoring the new behaviour until it is established. Include the new work habit on your daily 'to do' list for several weeks and reward yourself for sticking to it.

8 Find ways of providing timely reminders for those newly introduced routines that will not occur on a daily basis. If you use an electronic means of managing your commitments, you might employ the recurring appointment facility to prompt you at the appropriate times. Alternatively, you could use one of the many apps for phone or smartwatch that allow the user to enter habit-building goals, to receive timely reminders and to track progress towards making new habits automatic. Some of these include the possibility of support from other users or penalties for lapses.

9 Make use of checklists, forms and templates to reduce the mental effort involved in completing routine tasks.

10 Don't try to take on too much at once. Be satisfied with incremental steps, nurturing new habits until you are convinced they are established before turning your attention elsewhere.

Organize your decision making

Decisions inevitably come before action. If you suffer from indecisiveness or poor decision making, it will have an effect on the quality of your personal organization. And if you are fussing over decisions that don't need to be taken or that could be delegated to somebody else, then you will have less time and energy for the things that matter.

We are faced with decisions every day of our lives. Many are so routine as to have become habitual, requiring little conscious thought, but may be elevated in complexity under certain circumstances. Other decisions consume large amounts of time and emotional energy, and handling them effectively is a significant part of being organized.

If you're regularly faced with multiple decisions, you may find it helpful to get a handle on them by sorting them according to the following A–D grouping.

A At the simplest level are those decisions where the appropriate course of action is clear and upon which you are able to act immediately. Such decisions can be dealt with quickly and set aside.

B A closely allied second group consists of those decisions that are rightfully the responsibility of somebody else or which may be delegated to another party. This is not simply a matter of getting them off your own plate, but of placing authority and responsibility where it can best be exercised. (See Chapter 5 for more on delegation.)

C A third grouping is of those issues where further information is needed in order to make a decision. As an organized decision-maker you need to set that process in train – identifying from where the information will be obtained as well as determining what analysis of it may be required. Of course, information can be the cause of so-called 'analysis paralysis'. Either there is insufficient information to make an informed decision – often an excuse used to justify procrastination – or there is so much that the person responsible for the decision is overwhelmed. There is a fear element to information gathering too. On the one hand lies the fear that acquiring further information may throw up additional complications, while on the other is the equally damaging fear that if you stop information gathering you may miss an essential nugget that would set you on the right track. You need to keep data acquisition in proportion to the importance of the issue to be decided, and learn to recognize the point at which you have obtained sufficient information to define and weigh the options adequately, without tipping over into additional work, producing rapidly declining benefits.

D The final grouping is of those issues for which you have all the necessary information, but where it needs to be reflected upon before a decision or recommendation is finalized. There may be implications for other activities, for example, or longer term dimensions to be considered. Clearly, this shouldn't be used as an excuse for procrastination, and the time taken to ponder the issue will depend on both its complexity and the window of opportunity for making the decision. However, there is little doubt that letting your unconscious brain chew away at an issue can help reveal the bigger picture and uncover strands that may not have been apparent through rigid focus on achieving a swift outcome.

There are four parts to making any serious decision:

1 Clarify the who, the what and the how
This is best accomplished by asking yourself some questions. For example:

- Why do I need to make this decision?
- What are the goals I wish to achieve?
- What are the potential benefits and risks?
- Who will have responsibility for the decision?
- What information do I need to make this decision?
- How reliable is the information I have already?

- Is there any available reference point on how similar situations may have been tackled previously?
- What will happen if I do nothing?
- What are the implications if I make the wrong decision?
- Who do I need to consult or involve?
- What is the timescale? Is speed an important factor?
- What resources are available to me?

2 Identify the available options

Try to avoid any evaluation at this point, as doing so often results in unhelpful short circuits. In the process of identifying options, a superficially attractive one pops up and the focus moves away from exploration of all possibilities and towards justifying why this particular solution should be chosen. Even with decisions that require a speedy response it is worth taking a little time to ensure you have identified all the possible options before you start to evaluate them.

3 Weigh the pros and cons of each option

For complex decisions there are a number of tools that can assist analysis of information and evaluation of options, but such techniques go beyond the scope of this book. A simple balance sheet strategy will do the trick for more straightforward decisions. For each identified option, draw a line down the middle of a sheet of paper, listing the pros on one side and the cons on the other. Keep the goals of the exercise and the questions you asked yourself earlier clearly in front of you as you do this. Don't treat the pros and cons as if they all carry equal weight. You may want to give each a weighting on, say, a one to ten scale. But remember that you cannot expect to come to a conclusion simply by allocating and adding up weightings. Some points may have absolute rather than relative significance. A single point against may be of such weight that it eliminates all the points in favour. Beware also of what may seem to be overwhelming pros. The novelty value of some options may lead to the cons not being adequately explored.

4 Reduce the options to the point that you are able to make a choice

Some options will have been immediately dismissed by failing to meet the goals or having overwhelming points against them. For those that remain, you need to take account of risk surrounding their implementation. How likely is it that factors beyond your control may affect the successful implementation of the decision? And what is the balance of risk against potential gain? Also consider elements such as how the decision may be sold to those who have to implement it.

The process is seldom quite as straightforward as presented above. You should keep in mind the following potential impediments to effectiveness:

- **Fear and anxiety**

  Fear, as we have already seen, is a factor in procrastination. Decisions are often postponed or referred elsewhere out of fear of making a mistake. Anxiety about the process of implementing a decision may be just as important as choosing the right course of action. You may know what is the right thing to do, but the prospect of carrying it out is frightening. Possibly it holds the prospect of unpleasant encounters with others. Difficult decisions to do with people – disciplinary matters for example – are often bucked for this reason.

  It isn't just fear or anxiety that can prevent you from taking the right decision or acting upon it. Often we may be led to less than desirable outcomes by wholly laudable feelings such as sympathy and desire not to hurt the feelings of another.

- **Unconscious bias and gut instinct**

  When considering options, a common pitfall is to give greater weight to those that confirm our existing views. This so-called 'confirmation bias' can lead to potentially better options being overlooked. We're also inclined to take short cuts to a decision based on what we label as gut instinct when thorough analysis of the available information is really called for. Gut feeling does have a role to play in determining whether a decision is the right one but, except when the outcome is unimportant, it shouldn't be an alternative to proper analysis.

- **Inappropriate levels of effort**
  Many of the decisions we take simply do not warrant a great deal of effort, but even trivial decisions have an energy and attention cost which may be as debilitating as that for significantly more important matters. When choosing between alternatives of equal merit in a matter of just everyday significance, all that is necessary is to get to a satisfactory solution. Agonizing over the choice simply wastes valuable time and mental resources, and is an instance where the 80:20 rule needs to come into play. With other decisions, however, it's necessary to put in the time and effort to reach the very best possible conclusion. It's important to be clear which decisions require such an unreserved approach, and which require a solution that is just satisfactory.

- **The behaviour of others**
  Some decisions are purely personal, affecting only the individual making the choice, but, regardless of the environment in which they are taken, they will for the most part impact on others who will come with their full quota of prejudices, hobby horses and baggage. Others may need to be convinced of the benefits and perhaps to take ownership of the decision. So, actually taking the decision may not be the point at which the job finishes, rather the point at which it starts. It is often then a matter of communicating the decision and gaining the commitment of others, and this is where a lot of good decisions come unstuck. Communicating the decision is a selling job and the principles of effective persuasion apply:

  - Approach the task from your audience's point of view. Address their aspirations and fears.

  - Establish credibility by demonstrating a clear plan for the implementation of the decision.

- Sell the benefits of the decision rather than dwelling too much on the reasons for it.

- Anticipate any objections that may be raised and prepare convincing responses to them.

- **Temptation to avoid the decision**
You should remember that not taking a decision is, in itself, a decision and subject your inclination to some serious questioning. Is it anxiety that is prompting you, a genuine lack of available information or a judgement that the benefits of not making the decision outweigh the risks of making it?

 Decisions generally imply change, and many of us have a tendency to stick with the status quo, but research has shown that we are far more likely to regret the things we have not done than the actions we have taken.

- **Failure to move on**
Recognize that you can never get it right all the time, particularly when there are people involved. At the time you make the decision, its implementation lies in the future. Circumstances may change for reasons you couldn't have predicted at the time you made the decision, and because of that you do need to keep the consequences of decisions under review. But having chosen the best option, you need to implement it and move on, without constantly revisiting the options to worry whether you have made the right choice.

There are numerous apps for tablet and smartphone aimed at assisting users to choose between different courses of action. Typically they involve identifying important criteria, giving weightings to each, assessing possible outcomes and weighing pros and cons of alternative decisions. They may introduce greater rigour into the process, but the user needs to remain on the ball. Sloppy thinking in, for example, determining weightings is liable to result in less than satisfactory outcomes. It also has to be said that some of the apps are very gimmicky.

Summary points

Effective organization of your workload will be improved if you are able to:

- recognize those tasks which place the greatest demands on you and schedule them when you are at your most energetic;
- fit the task to the time you have available;
- build up positive work habits and eliminate negative ones;
- take a systematic approach to decisions.

04
Organize information

- Does the amount of incoming information you are required to deal with seem to be constantly growing?
- Do you find yourself going over the same material more than once without seeming to take it in?
- Would you like to be able to read faster while maintaining or improving your comprehension?
- Do you have difficulty keeping up to date with the reading and research you feel is necessary for effective performance of your job?
- Do colleagues bombard you with forwarded emails, reports and copies of other material that you don't need?
- Do you find yourself unable to decide what to do with documents and messages you receive?
- Do you put items to one side to be dealt with later?
- Do you retain magazines, reports and web references intending to read them, but never get around to it?
- Are you plagued by junk mail?
- Do you find difficulty locating a piece of information which you know is somewhere within a particular book or report?

If you haven't answered yes to any of these, then you are a pretty unusual being in today's workplace. Recent surveys have shown that throughout the developed world, people are struggling to cope with the vast quantities of information they are required to handle in their jobs and that widespread stress and productivity decline are a result.

In this chapter we will look at a systematic approach towards handling incoming information. We will examine ways to reduce the volume of what comes your way, and techniques to help you read, sort and assimilate it more efficiently.

Identify the important information

Some information is immediately recognizable as junk. Other items scream their importance. But it isn't always simple to separate with certainty the vital from the marginal. Use the following questions to help determine the value of whatever information comes your way:

- Does this information relate to a key element of my job?
- Would I choose to receive or keep this information if I had to pay for it?
- What is the worst that would happen if I ignored it?
- Is it information that I need at this point in time? If not, can I access it easily should I want it in future?
- Eighty per cent of the value comes from 20 per cent of the information. Is this item in the top 20 per cent?

You cannot be sure of getting it right every time, but resist the temptation to deal with this uncertainty by a strategy of 'if in doubt, treat it as important'. Information perfection – always having exactly the right information available at the right time – is not possible. While the availability of good information is important to the effective discharge of your job, more information will not guarantee better performance. Beyond a certain point, additional information will have a declining marginal value, and information has no value at all if there is so much of it that it cannot be properly interpreted and understood. So, recognize that you have no hope of taking in everything, focus on the important, and accept that your judgement will be imperfect. Remember also the need to discriminate between the urgent and the important. Items requiring a speedy response may assume a greater importance than they deserve. An unimportant matter which has been left unattended for several days does not become any more important because its deadline is approaching. It simply becomes more urgent.

Adopt a systematic approach

There is a common myth, perpetuated by some time-management programmes, that every item of information should be handled only once. It doesn't work like that in the real world. For a variety of reasons, you might need to come back to a document. An item may genuinely need to be mulled over or put together with other information before you can make a sensible decision upon it. It may be more efficient to deal with some items in context with others on the same subject. What about the document or email which makes you angry? Although a response fired off immediately may do something for your blood pressure, you are likely to produce a more effective reply, and one less likely to escalate confrontation, if you wait until you have cooled off. Some items may need repeated handling in the process of drafting a complex document. If it is possible to handle a document only once, then this is clearly what you should aim for, but don't become too hung up on the 'one touch' approach. Ensure that no document or message goes back onto the pile, and that every item receives a positive action on the first touch. This action should be one of the following five Ds, summarized in Figure 4.1.

Discard

The quickest way to become bogged down with information is by wasting time and energy reading and pondering material of little or

Figure 4.1   The five Ds

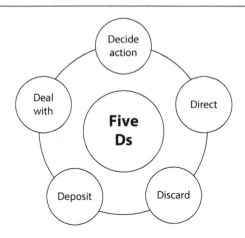

no benefit to you. So, the first question to ask yourself is 'Do I want this at all?' It should be quickly apparent if an item has no use for you, but we are often reluctant to consider the bin until we have waded through a document. There is also a tendency to put to one side documents that one is unsure about. There they form a mounting pile with other items, gathering dust or clogging up your inbox – occasionally being revisited in half-hearted attempts to clear the backlog. Remember that most information has a limited shelf life. A useful rule of thumb is – if it doesn't seem valuable today it isn't likely to tomorrow.

Deal with

Provided that you are able to do so quickly and effectively, you should deal with items when they first come to you. An immediate action on a document or message is satisfying and stress-relieving. It also means that you will not have to spend time refreshing your memory before you can act upon it in the future. Where it is not possible to deal with an item immediately, then at least decide what action you will take and when.

Decide future action

When dealing with paper, never return an item to the pile. Make sure you have a system for bringing forward items on which you will need to act, and make a point of noting the action required, or the possible options, on the document or a sticky note attachment. A concertina file marked with the dates of the month makes a useful 'bring forward' device. Place the item in the compartment corresponding to the date when you wish to revisit it.

Depending on your software, you can adopt a similar approach with email. If you're using an application such as Outlook with a 'flag for follow up' facility, you can simply tag the message and choose when to receive a reminder about it. Other applications may not have the ability to issue timed reminders, but they will generally have some facility for flagging or tagging messages. Designate one of these tags for follow up, and you can easily run a search to call up all those messages you need to return to. Remember to remove the tag once you have dealt with the message. Alternatively, you can set up a special folder for all messages that have actions pending, but you must remember to visit it regularly.

You will need to exert some discipline in respect of items marked for future action:

- Do not use it to avoid one of the other four Ds.
- Do not move items on beyond the day you have originally set for action.
- If you have a 'to read' file, don't let it become a general dumping ground.

Direct

Don't send items to others just to get them off your own desk or out of your inbox, or because you don't know what to do with them. You will only add to other people's information burden and possibly fill the bins of others more quickly than your own. Think about why you are redirecting the item and what you want the other person to do with it. A brief note will help them to assimilate and act upon it more quickly.

Deposit

Storing an item in whatever form of filing system is not an action to take because you don't know what else to do with it. Be sparing in what you file. This particularly applies to the filing of paper documents, which tends to be labour and space intensive. You can afford to be more generous in the filing of digital documents, but even here a general policy of retaining material just in case can lead to more protracted retrieval tasks. We will look at ground rules for filing in Chapter 7.

Avoid overload

However effective you become at handling the stuff, you will not achieve all that is possible unless you also take steps to reduce the volume of information that daily competes for your attention. Even if you only glance at the majority of it, you may be wasting considerable time and effort.

There is a tendency to feel powerless in the face of a relentless flow of documents, emails, calls, texts and instant messages. But there are things that can be done to retain a greater degree of control.

The first step harks back to Chapter 1 of this book. If you are to have any hope of separating the wheat from the chaff, it is essential that you are clear about your objectives and can differentiate between the important and the trivial. Once you're able to do this there are several ways in which you can set about reducing your overload. Here are some possibilities.

Opt-out

In a number of countries the process of opting out from legitimate but unwanted communication has been eased by the introduction of stricter data protection regulations governing how personal information may be stored and used. Express consent is an increasingly common requirement before personal email addresses and phone numbers can be used for promotional purposes, and unsubscribing has become more straightforward. Unfortunately, many of us are still careless with our permissions and ignore opportunities to stem the inflow of unnecessary material. You may be able to streamline your inbox by examining the range of regular messages, newsletters, updates and offers you receive, and unsubscribing from those that offer negligible value.

If interactions with social networking sites are a factor in your overload, ask yourself some serious questions about the place of this activity. Does social networking play a valuable part in the business with which you are involved or is it imposing unduly upon your working life? Are you using it as a shield to avoid other tasks?

Filter

When searching or browsing for information on the internet, remember that you cannot possibly handle more than the tiniest proportion of the available information. Much of what is out there will be of poor or dubious quality, requiring further effort to interpret it or verify its reliability. Therefore, stick with quality sites. There will be further tips on assessing quality in Chapter 8.

Make certain that you are using the junk mail filters included with your email or antivirus software as fully as possible to eliminate total junk and malicious mailings.

Disconnect

Constant connectedness is a very serious impediment to effective working, and can greatly add to your sense of overload. One of the great benefits of most modern forms of communication should be their time independence. We should have the ability to choose when to respond to emails, texts and voicemail messages, but many of us handle them in the same way we would an old-style landline call – reading and responding as they arrive and disrupting other activity in the process. Restricting the number of occasions during the day when you will read and respond to messages can provide a major boost to productivity. We will look further at how you might take more control of this area of communication in the section on overcoming distractions and interruptions in Chapter 5.

Delete

Global estimates indicate that significantly more than 50 per cent of email traffic is spam. However, by no means all unsolicited mail is total junk. A fair proportion is likely to be from organizations you have dealt with previously and indeed may do so again, but it is mail that you neither need nor desire at this particular time. Nevertheless, the inclination is to read it and possibly even retain it just in case. The demand on your time occasioned by each incidence of communication is small, but together they can add up to a large imposition. If you are struggling with the volume of incoming mail, hitting the delete button straight away is likely to make a deal more sense. Anything of value is liable to be the subject of further communication. Indeed, you can expand this approach into a general one of ignoring and deleting most incoming information unless there appears to be a good reason to do otherwise.

Cooperate

Remember that clear requests are more likely to get clear answers. If you are bogged down by an overabundance of forwarded messages or garbled communication, it may be that you haven't specified clearly enough what you require from others.

When you're not sure what to do with a document or who may need sight of an email, the easiest solution is to engage in multiple copying and send it to everybody who might conceivably have use for the information therein. You have achieved two things – the offending item is off your hands, and you have also absolved yourself from any responsibility for failure to communicate. However, you have added to the information burden of others and have not necessarily communicated anything of value. If you aim to protect yourself by over-copying to colleagues, they are likely to respond in the same way.

There may be instances where several members of a workgroup can cooperate to relieve their collective information burden. If, for example, you all regularly have to read and assimilate complex documents, it may be possible to take it in turns for one lead reader to provide a summary for the others, thus speeding and assisting their assimilation of the document.

Read more efficiently

The speed and efficiency with which you can assimilate incoming information is a significant factor in your ability to organize your workload. It has been estimated that people in information-intensive jobs may spend up to a third of their working day in activities involving reading, and yet most of us are not as efficient readers as we might be. The average reading speed is between 200 and 300 words a minute. With some simple techniques and practice this can be raised to 500+ without detriment to your understanding. Slow reading speeds are not particularly a function of education or intelligence. Many able and well-educated people read at or below the average speed. Even if you already read quickly, there is generally scope for improvement. It is a myth that only by reading slowly can we expect to understand material. Better comprehension can go hand in hand with faster reading.

The easiest way to estimate your current reading speed is to use one of the numerous online reading-speed tests. Alternatively, choose an appropriate passage at least a page in length that you haven't previously read. Try to read it at a normal pace consistent with understanding the content and take an accurate note of the time it takes you. Then, estimate the length of the passage by multiplying the average number of words per line by the number of lines in the passage. The number of words in the passage multiplied by 60 and subsequently divided by the time taken in seconds will give you your reading speed in words per minute.

Why do we read slowly?

When we read, our eyes do not move continuously across the page, but rather hop several words at a time through the material. It is during the stationary period (fixation) at the end of each hop that the reading occurs; and it is, of course, the brain which does the reading rather than the eyes. In simple terms, we might think of the eyes as a still camera taking a series of shots which the brain then interprets. The main reasons for slow reading speed are:

- limited number of words encompassed in each fixation;
- fixations of longer duration than necessary;
- involuntary or deliberate back-skipping over material already read.

A fourth factor in slow reading is a tendency to mentally hear the words as we read. This is known as sub-vocalization and is believed to originate from the approach used when we first learn to read – actually speaking the words aloud. The problem with sub-vocalization is that it restricts us to little more than the speed of the spoken voice, which is typically around 150–200 words a minute. Sub-vocalization can be greatly diminished if never entirely eliminated.

Increasing your speed

There are numerous books, courses and applications for computer, tablet and smartphone that aim to help increase reading speed and understanding. Some offer seemingly fantastic advances within a very short time, but I would be inclined to dismiss the more outlandish claims. The two most frequently used techniques for overcoming the issues associated with slow reading are meta-guiding and rapid serial visual presentation.

Meta-guiding is the oldest speed-reading technique and involves some form of pacing mechanism which forces your eyes to move on and cuts down distraction and back-skipping. At its simplest it's a matter of using an index finger or the blunt end of a pencil and moving it swiftly across the page just below the line of text you are reading. The aim is to maintain a pace above that which feels comfortable and prevent your eyes going back over what you've already read. Of course, technology has now taken over from the pencil and there are numerous 'faster reading' apps that will present you with scrolling lines of text, the pace of which can be individually determined.

The second common technique is rapid serial visual presentation (RSVP) whereby single words from a passage are flashed sequentially in front of the reader, once again at a speed that can be increased as the user becomes accustomed to a particular pace. Fans of this means of speed enhancement claim that it cuts out the need for the eyes to move and thereby reduces the amount of time for each fixation.

Anyone wishing to locate faster reading applications will have no difficulty finding a host of examples. Reviews will help you separate the good from the indifferent. There are examples both free and paid for, offering varying levels of sophistication and guidance. Some of the most useful allow you to use your own documents for practice, rather than random passages presented by the application.

Increasing your reading speed will take time and patience, but there are further techniques you can employ almost immediately that will have a bearing on both speed and understanding.

Preview for increased understanding

We read much more quickly and effectively if we are slotting information into a known framework. A few moments spent establishing that framework can pay significant dividends. The approach which follows assumes you are setting out to read a substantial document such as a book, periodical or report. It can be adapted for shorter documents and applies as much to electronic documents as paper ones.

1 Before starting on the main text, skim through the Contents page, Introduction and Summary (if there is one) or Conclusions.

2 Next, zip through the document, establishing an appreciation of the main structure and argument. Look particularly for section or chapter summaries. They are excellent for getting quickly to the guts of a document. Failing that, read the first and last paragraph of each section or chapter. These will often introduce and summarize the arguments contained therein.

3 Now, when you move to read the document properly, you will be filling in the gaps rather than starting with a blank sheet. You will know which are the parts you need to concentrate on, and which you can blast through or skip altogether.

Vary your pace

It goes without saying that texts vary in their levels of difficulty, but many people maintain the same pace regardless of what they are reading. Even within a document there will be some sections which are more difficult to absorb than others. Don't be afraid to slow down where the text requires it, and to power through the easier passages. You shouldn't neglect the fact that, while reading may be a chore in some contexts, in others it is a source of great enjoyment. Reading a novel, poem or play is not a matter of blasting through the text, hoovering up facts. There are often passages to be savoured, nuances to be appreciated and leisurely contemplation of meaning that may be entirely at odds with a speed reading approach.

Focus on what is important

At some point in most documents there will be digressions from the main argument, things which you already know, things you don't need to know and straightforward padding. The best way to approach any reading task is with the question 'What do I need from this?' foremost in your mind. You will read more quickly and remember more if you can focus on the elements which are necessary for you in whatever task you have to fulfil. Don't approach the printed word with too much reverence. The writer does not necessarily know any more than you do on the subject.

Develop scanning techniques

When you need to find a particular piece of information in a paper-based document, you can move to it quickly by scanning. Focus your attention solely on the information you wish to locate and let your eyes follow your finger as you run it rapidly down the centre of each page from top to bottom. This process should be considerably faster than your paced reading, and if you are focused on the information you want to locate, it should leap out at you when you get to the relevant part of the document. You will improve with practice. Of course, scanning is no substitute for using an index where one exists, and scanning is generally unnecessary when seeking specific information in an electronic document. It is quicker and more reliable to use the search facility, entering a relevant word or phrase.

Be selective about what you read

Never try to read everything that lands on your desk or in your inbox. That way lies madness. You need to be ruthlessly selective and stick to those things which add value to your role. And remember – people who put reading matter aside for an indeterminate time in the future when they will be less busy are destined to be forever disappointed.

Manage your memory

The value of what you read declines pretty rapidly if you can't remember it. Indeed, if you do nothing to assist your memory you'll forget up to 80 per cent of what you have read within 24 hours. And it's not just about written information. Many of us are plagued by inadequate recall in all manner of settings. Remembering names and faces or where we have put things tend to rank highest on the frustration index, but there are numerous other examples where memory lets us down. Paying attention to the way our memories work and employing some simple techniques can make a significant difference to this notoriously fallible aspect of our personal organization.

Throughout our waking lives we are bombarded with a multitude of stimuli and it is neither desirable nor necessary for us to remember all that we perceive. Our brains engage in a process of selective filtering without which we would be overwhelmed. Only information we deem important and relevant makes it through to our long-term memory. Often the things we 'forget' are lost because we had never properly registered them in the first place. When I discover that I can't remember the name of somebody to whom I've just been introduced, it may be because my mind was too busy rehearsing what I might say to them to properly take their name on board. Similarly, the loss of my keys may be down to the fact that, when I walked into the house and put them down, I had other more pressing issues on my mind.

Of course, we have tried and tested methods of recording information to spare our brains the conflicting clutter and the inevitable loss of information that would result from simply relying on our memories. For millennia we have written things down, and in today's world we have the advantage of unprecedented access to almost the sum total of human knowledge at the click of a mouse or tap of a screen. Frequently, it isn't so much a matter of us needing actively to retain a particular piece of information as knowing where that information may be accessed. Additionally, gadgetry offers timely prompts to aid our fallible memories. But external props will only take us so far, and we need to give our memories a run out if they are to serve us well.

Here are 10 strategies aimed at more effective remembering:

1 You will assist your memory if you take account of the level of recall you are likely to require. For some information, it will be sufficient for you to remember simply that it exists and where to find it. With other information you will need a grasp of the general subject and main ideas. At the highest level you may need to recall information in detail or even verbatim.

2 Read with a question in your mind. What do I want to achieve from this? How does it fit into what I know already? All learning and remembering is a process of association.

3 Try to see the overall pattern to what you are reading. We remember much better if we can see the general structure and the broad ideas into which the detail fits.

4 Distinguish between recognition and recall. Recognition, the process of remembering with assistance from an external stimulus, is much easier than pure recall.

5 Use the information in some way. Summarize it in your own words, make margin notes as you read, communicate the information to others, or act upon it.

6 Review important information to fix it in your long-term memory. You will gain the most advantage by quickly reviewing material shortly after acquiring it (10 to 15 minutes) and again a day later. Experts recommend further review after a week and a month for reliable long-term recall.

7 Your memory for the location of things you need to access readily will be greatly assisted if you keep like things together. This may seem an overly simplistic statement but, while we expect to find things logically arranged in shops and libraries, we often neglect appropriate groupings of objects within our homes and offices. Make sure too that files, either of the physical or digital variety, are grouped in a rational hierarchy.

8 Designate habitual locations for things that you are frequently inclined to lose, such as keys.

9 Make up your own mnemonics for hard to remember sequences. As a child you may have been taught little jingles for remembering such things as: the notes on the treble clef, the position of planets in the solar system and the sequence of colours in the rainbow (Richard Of York Gave Battle In Vain). It's not too difficult to invent your own to help with tricky sequences in your adult life.

10 If you have difficulty remembering names, make sure that when you are first introduced to a person, you use their name more than once in the ensuing conversation. Making conscious associations may also help to fix their name in your mind. If you are introduced to a Brian Roper, for example, you might make a visual image of him tied up with rope. The more bizarre the image more likely you are to remember it. It's especially useful if you can make an association between a predominant facial feature of the person in question and their name. Sometimes this is a real struggle, but even the effort of trying to make an association helps to register a person's name in your memory.

Activity – ask yourself

1   What steps could I usefully take to deal more effectively with incoming information?

2   What, if any, strategies should I apply to boost my reading speed and understanding?

3   How might I set about improving recall of important information?

Enter any resulting objectives in your master list of things to do.

Summary points

Dealing effectively with information is a matter of:

- separating the important information from the junk;
- maintaining a systematic approach with all incoming Information;
- taking steps to reduce information overload;
- building up your reading speed and comprehension;
- using memory techniques and review to assist your recall.

05
Organize the way you work with others

Much of our working day is spent in some form of interaction with others. The way you approach these interactions can have a considerable impact on your effectiveness. In this chapter we shall look at meetings, delegation, overcoming distractions and interruptions and learning to say no.

A strategy for meetings

The time-wasting potential of meetings is immense. In many organizations you can spend hours every week in meetings that achieve very little. But for all that we moan about them, we keep on holding the things and attending them. Why?

People attend meetings for reasons other than to make decisions. Meetings cultivate a sense of one's importance – closeness to the wheels of power. They are an opportunity to make an impression on your colleagues. Not being invited may smack of exclusion. I have known people, left out of meetings that had almost negligible relevance to them, become incandescent over what they perceived as deliberate downgrading attempts. There is also a social element to meetings, and they can be less demanding than some other forms of work activity. Once you are in the meeting you're cocooned, safe from phone calls, interruptions and the tough problems that inhabit your inbox. OK, so meetings are boring, but you can play a few mind games with colleagues or just let your attention wander.

Why do we hold meetings? Meetings are held to:

- impart information;
- elicit views;
- provide updates on progress;
- stimulate new ideas;
- work collectively on joint projects;
- motivate a group;
- plan strategy;
- reach decisions.

There are more effective ways of passing on information than dragging people together and subjecting them to one of those verbal memo meetings where only the senior person speaks and everybody else sits mute. There are also non-meeting ways of consulting and eliciting views. The creative or brainstorming meeting has long been seen as a way of exploring new solutions to problems, but studies have shown that frequently people are more creative when working individually. Similarly, one-to-one reinforcement and coaching can often achieve more than a motivational team meeting, and the non-challenging culture (groupthink) developed by some meetings may not favour good decisions.

So, in the face of all this, whenever the prospect of a meeting comes up, the first question to ask yourself is: Do we need a meeting at all? Unfortunately that question isn't asked often enough. In many organizations, meetings go ahead at regular intervals regardless of whether they are really needed. Business expands to fill the agenda and you have all the ingredients of a classic talking shop.

Assuming that you decide a meeting really is necessary, what can you do to ensure that it achieves its purpose without devouring too much of the participants' time? Unproductive meetings generally fall down on aspects of planning and management.

Inadequate planning

There may be no agenda, a poorly prepared one, or no clear purpose to the meeting. Information needed to make sensible decisions may not have been produced, or participants may have failed to read it in advance.

Poor management

There may be inadequate control of timing, failure to keep discussion on the agenda, inability to control people intent on riding their pet hobby horses, inability to draw conclusions out of the discussion.

Here are some pointers aimed at overcoming these and other meeting problems.

Ten points to remember when calling a meeting

1 Frame the agenda as clearly as possible. Identify the specific questions the meeting needs to address rather than setting open-ended topics.

2 Indicate a target time allowance for each agenda item and stick to it as closely as you can.

3 Limit attendance to those who have something to contribute on the matters under discussion and the authority to implement decisions. Generally speaking, the more people there are at a meeting, the longer it will take.

4 Schedule meetings immediately before lunch or at the end of the day. People's anxiety to get away will override their verbosity.

5 Try not to schedule meetings in your own work area. You will find it harder to get away from any post-meeting hangers-on.

6 Start the meeting at the scheduled time. Waiting for late-comers encourages them to repeat the misdemeanour and irritates those who have arrived on time.

7 Don't allow discussion to be sidetracked onto matters not on the agenda. If they are important they can be dealt with at a subsequent meeting.

8 Don't waste time discussing matters where there is inadequate information to make a decision. Agree responsibility for obtaining and reporting the necessary information and postpone the discussion to a future date.

9 Avoid the practice of Any Other Business at the end of meetings if at all possible. It is often used by people too lazy to prepare an item properly for the agenda, and can result in bad decisions made on the basis of inadequate consideration. It can also kick into touch all your efforts at timing discussion.

10 Ensure that as soon as possible after the meeting, a record of the outcomes is prepared. The quicker it is done, the easier the task. Detailed minutes are generally unnecessary, and only give people something to argue over at the start of the next meeting. Action notes are more useful. They should include: a) what the meeting agreed; b) who has responsibility for actioning those agreements; and c) dates by which they should be actioned.

Ten points to remember when attending a meeting

1 Make sure beforehand that you know what the meeting is aiming to achieve. If the aim doesn't seem clear, question the convenor about it. This may have the effect of clarifying objectives, leading to a more productive meeting, or demonstrating that a meeting isn't actually needed.

2 Ask to be excused from any meeting which does not appear to have any relevance to you. You have to be wise to the politics of this. If your boss is the one calling the meeting, diplomacy may require that you go. Often, however, the convenor simply hasn't given sufficient thought to meeting membership. Questions like 'What are you hoping I will be able to contribute?' can lead them to think again.

3 If only one item in a meeting is relevant to you, ask whether it can be placed near the beginning of the agenda so that you can be spared the rest of the meeting. Be aware, though, that this tactic sometimes sparks a bidding war on the part of others similarly affected.

4 Always read the agenda and any papers before a meeting and, without taking up an inflexible position, clarify your thoughts as to what you would like to achieve from the meeting.

5 If you expect your arguments to meet with some opposition, a little subtle lobbying in advance may be useful. Other participants may not have given the meeting much advance thought, and people are more inclined to stick with a view that they take into the room than they are to be won over by something they hear during the meeting. Handle lobbying carefully though. If the other person sees your approach as an attempt to exert undue influence, you risk actually turning them away from your point of view.

6 Think in advance about what you will settle for if you don't get what you want. Most people will not have thought about a fallback position. Skilfully presented – that is before it is apparent to everyone that you have lost the argument – it can be a disarming way of getting at least a substantial part of what you want.

7 Don't overcommit yourself. Meetings are a bit like auctions. In the to and fro of discussion it's easy to get carried away and make undertakings you later regret. There's a natural wish to make a good impression in front of colleagues, but don't let yourself be tempted into taking on too many responsibilities or offering unrealistic target dates for completion of work.

8 If you find yourself locked into excessively long meetings, arrange for an 'important' appointment, or vital interruption, which will require you to leave before the end. Don't do it too often, or you will arouse suspicions.

9 You can help a weak chairperson by summarizing the arguments of others and pulling the threads of a discussion together to

facilitate decisions. By all means draw people's attention to overruns on time, but take care to ensure that you are not a guilty party. We tend to overestimate the time that other people have been talking and underestimate our own loquacity.

10 Try to set some regular times when you are available for meetings attendance and make them known. If you are able to make this work, it can help prevent meetings breaking up your working week in such a way that you are unable to get to those tasks which require concentrated activity over a number of hours.

Remote meetings

The prevalence of online meetings was on the rise before the global pandemic of 2020 but, for obvious reasons, has increased exponentially since then. Video conferencing offers a major time-saving advantage over the traditional meeting in that participants are spared the need to travel, but remote meetings share most of the difficulties experienced in the face-to-face variety, and introduce a couple of additional ones. Let's examine these briefly along with some possible solutions.

The first drawback concerns technical issues. Some participants may not be adequately familiar with the hardware and software they are using or may be hooked up to less reliable internet connections. Sometimes the software itself will refuse to play ball. Technical issues frequently result in immense frustration for all participants even if the particular problem only affects one or two.

The second regular complaint about online meetings is that they are even more tedious than traditional ones. There's no doubt that it can be hard to remain engaged while staring at a screen for a couple of hours, especially when lengthy presentations are being made and you are not required to contribute. In meetings where some members are physically present while others are remote there may be an additional tendency for the online members to be overlooked.

Online meetings feel less natural and some participants may experience a degree of self-consciousness at being 'on camera'. This somewhat artificial atmosphere may be exacerbated by hardware limitations such as the phenomenon whereby participants appear not to be making eye contact, the result of them being filmed by a camera at a slightly different angle to the screen on which their attention is focused. Studies have also shown that participants in a video conference have to work harder to interpret information and communicative nuances than would be the case in a face-to-face meeting.

In the light of these difficulties, it has been suggested that in situations where there is no need for face-to-face contact or for visual images to be displayed, an audio conference call can be less problematic and just as effective as a video conference. Nevertheless, video conferencing is undoubtedly here to stay, and there are simple steps you can take to make it a more enjoyable and productive experience.

Ten steps towards more effective remote meetings

1 Ensure in advance that every meeting participant is familiar with the platform being used and standard meeting etiquette. For example, they should know how to indicate a wish to speak, and commit to muting their microphones when not speaking.

2 Have a fallback option in the form of an alternative platform in the event of technical problems with your first-choice conferencing application.

3 Encourage participants to join meetings ahead of the scheduled start so that time isn't wasted troubleshooting.

4 Make sure the aims of the meeting are clearly communicated in advance, that it is well structured and has a tight agenda. These are standard points, but they are even more important for remote meetings than those where everyone is in the same room.

5 Allocate preparatory tasks in advance of the meeting and give people roles to fulfil during it.

6 Don't hold remote meetings too frequently. Often the decision to have an online meeting is a lazy option and may prove less productive than alternatives.

7 Use a variety of media for communicating information – slides, whiteboard, graphic presentation – and use third-party add-ons that may enhance the meeting, but make sure you are completely familiar with them before going live.

8 Ask questions of participants during the meeting to ensure that everyone is still engaged; use live polling to elicit group responses and to reach decisions.

9 Present opportunities for participation, especially by inviting contributions from those who have hitherto been silent.

10 Record meetings for the benefit of those unable to attend, and seek genuine feedback after meetings conclude.

Alternatives to meetings

As noted at the beginning of this section there are better ways of doing some of the business that is traditionally reserved for meetings. Too often it is the default response for dealing with an issue, and one that may occupy many more person hours and be less effective than an alternative approach. It may be possible to achieve the desired ends without bringing a group of people together or adopting a 'one size fits all' approach to team business:

- For those elements of meetings that are to do with conveying information, a group email or an online presentation will often do the trick and, if steps are taken to set up question and feedback options accessible to all participants, then queries can be dealt with in a manner that doesn't prove a boring waste of time for more informed members of the group.

- Collaborative apps and cloud-based team software can remove many of the reasons for calling meetings. Responsibilities can be allocated, ideas shared, solutions to problems worked upon, progress towards team goals identified and documents revised collectively. Where the aim is to elicit views, a proposition can be made under a discussion thread started within an email group.

- Email and instant messaging often make for irritating interruptions to other work, but if used judiciously they can reduce the time that has to be spent in meetings by offering a simple and immediate means of sharing ideas and answering questions.

Activity – ask yourself

What steps could I take to limit unnecessary meetings and improve the effectiveness of meetings I am engaged in? Frame responses you wish to implement as objectives that can be entered in your master 'to do' list.

Delegate

CASE STUDY

Edward Newton reckons to work an average 58-hour week. The company he works for has been going through major changes recently and Edward's job has been closely associated with those changes. He is aware that he tries to do too many things himself and that some tasks could be passed on to other members of his team, but he feels that those he can trust are themselves overloaded. It's also his belief that, in the short term, the time taken to brief and coach somebody else would exceed the time he is currently spending on these tasks. His problem is exacerbated because, in a situation of change, he is unsure how long his workload will remain at the present level, and hence he is reluctant to pass on responsibilities only to take them back later. At the back of his mind there is even a slight worry that he may need his heavy workload to justify his existence in any future restructuring. From time to time he gets so overloaded that he simply has to dump jobs on colleagues with wholly insufficient briefing or assistance.

There are lots of Edwards in every area of work – people whose competence is being stretched to the limit by competition, change and restructuring. They are suffering from the catch-22 situation where they know they ought to delegate more but feel they haven't the time to do it properly. But for anybody who wants to get organized and stay on top of the job, delegation has to be part of the recipe.

The first important point about delegation is that it should not be a knee-jerk reaction to your own overload. It isn't just a matter of offloading tasks you don't want to do, but a contribution to overall productivity by placing responsibility and the necessary authority and resources where they can be discharged most effectively. You will have difficulty with delegation if you're not prepared to invest the time in setting arrangements up, if you can't trust your colleagues or if you cannot believe that anyone else is able to do the job as well as you.

At one time delegation was always seen in terms of tasks being passed to more junior colleagues, but in these days of flatter organizational structures, there is an increased tendency to think of sideways delegation – the movement of work between colleagues at the same or a similar level. This is really more about trading responsibilities than delegating them in the traditional sense. We all have differing skills and work preferences. If a colleague is able to fulfil an area of your responsibility more effectively than you, and you in turn can bring your skills to an aspect of his or her job, then it makes sense to cooperate. However, the fact that the arrangement is between colleagues at the same level should not be a reason for any less care in the setting-up process.

Five steps to effective delegation

1. Decide what you will delegate

The choice of responsibilities to delegate will normally centre on those things that others may do more quickly, more cheaply or more expertly than you, or tasks that can readily be performed within the context of another person's existing job. There will generally be core elements to your own job that you should not consider delegating.

2. Choose the right person

Beware of the natural tendency to load the willing horses or to delegate tasks only to those who have fulfilled similar work in the past. The reasons for delegation are not only about easing your own workload but about giving new development experiences to others.

3. Prepare the ground

You have to be ready to prepare colleagues for what you want them to do. Time to do this is often an issue, but it is a matter of short-term pain for long-term gain. If you don't set the arrangement up properly, you are likely to have disgruntled colleagues feeling they have been dumped on or people unclear about what is expected of them. You will need to set clear objectives using the SMART formula we discussed in Chapter 1. Let your colleague know the parameters of his or her authority and what support you will be able to provide.

4. Sell the benefits

It's important to look at these from the other person's point of view. There may be training and development benefits to him or her in taking on a new responsibility, enhancement of career prospects, variety and challenge, or opportunity to use particular skills. Be prepared to spend time talking to the person concerned, seeking responses to what you are proposing, and responding constructively. If your colleague can feel that the setting-up process is a collaborative one, he or she will be more committed to taking it on.

5. Stand back

Let the other person get on with it. One of the most common delegation problems is a tendency to interfere or reject the work because it is not being done in exactly the way you would have done it. You need to work hard to avoid this, particularly if you have been doing the job yourself for some time. You should make it clear that you are available to offer support, but that day-to-day responsibility is down to the person to whom you have delegated it. If you don't, it will remain essentially your responsibility, for which you have simply contracted out part of the donkey work. When problems occur they will wind up back on your plate, and your colleague will not achieve the development benefits that delegation can offer. Of course, the authority you delegate is not limitless, and the person taking on the responsibility should be aware of its limits, but he or she also needs the freedom to operate and sometimes to make mistakes and learn from them.

Activity - ask yourself

What tasks would it be possible for me to delegate in order to achieve better overall performance in my team? How might I set about delegating such tasks? Enter any resultant objectives in your master list.

Overcome distractions and interruptions

Interruptions and distractions impose heavily on our ability to organize work schedules. Not only is there the actual time lost through the interruption but, more importantly, the effort of getting back to the original task and refocusing attention. The extent to which we are distracted from our work has become much more acute in recent years as a result of technological advances. We live and work in a world where we are constantly connected, often simultaneously, to multiple communication vehicles – email, the web, mobile phone calls, texts and instant messaging – not to mention our face-to-face interactions with people and the impact of old-fashioned landline telecommunication. In many settings, this ever-present connectedness and the requirement to juggle tasks constantly is regarded as an essential aspect of working life, and multitasking has become the order of the day. But multitasking is not something that human beings are very good at. We may manage it well enough with a couple of activities where one is automatic, such as holding a conversation while driving. But you'll note that even this becomes appreciably more difficult if the driving task is elevated from the largely automatic; for example, when negotiating a complex junction. We all have limited capacity for simultaneous mental activity, and what really happens during supposed multitasking involving even relatively undemanding activities is that we rapidly switch our attention from one to the other. This constant shifting of focus has an energy cost that can severely limit our effectiveness, and it may also interfere with the business of processing information between short-term and long-term memory.

Additionally, interruptions and attempted multitasking disrupt momentum which can be hugely important when you are working on a demanding activity. One study conducted by Microsoft Research and the University of Illinois found that it can take up to 15 minutes to productively resume a challenging task when interrupted by something as simple as an email. It has been found that in some occupations workers are having to switch their attention every few minutes, and the detrimental effects of this are becoming so widely acknowledged that a new term – 'continuous partial attention syndrome' – is increasingly used to describe them.

Of course, not all distractions and interruptions are techno-logical in nature. Some are social, often by people who are them-selves engaged in procrastination over tasks they want to escape. You may even be the source of the distraction. One study claims that the proportion of distractions that are self-induced may be as high as 50 per cent. It is very easy to convince yourself that you just have to make a phone call, get a coffee, update your social media status or check your favourite blog, and you will be back on track in a few minutes. Once the pattern of work is disrupted, you find other 'pressing' chores and the minutes may stretch to an hour, after which time it is much harder to pick up the threads.

It has been suggested that individuals can train themselves to get back on track more quickly, but a better strategy has to be one of limiting the number of distractions and interruptions in the first place. Aim to cut out all bar the most urgent and important – those things that impinge on the key purpose of your job or the organ-ization you work for, and where the consequences of failure to give the matter your immediate attention may be of detriment to either.

The great benefit of email, voicemail and text messaging should be their time independence, and you will certainly be far more pro-ductive if you are able to deal with them at times of your choosing rather than when they arrive. Research has shown that people handle messages and other interruptions much more effectively if they occur at natural break points in the other activities they are carrying out. If it is possible for you to do so, set two or three times each day when you will routinely check and deal with calls and messages, and be disciplined about sticking to this routine.

Unfortunately, for many readers, this may seem like an un-achievable luxury. If you work in a culture where there is an expectation of immediate responses to calls and messages, it may feel almost impossible to free yourself from constant interruptions.

But if you want to get the important things done, it is essential that you look for ways to balance accessibility and productivity. You might like to consider ways of giving yourself email-free periods – times when you can work uninterrupted on tasks that require your complete attention. This might mean closing off all messages for a period or filtering them to ensure that only those requiring your immediate attention make it through. Exploring your email software settings and consulting the help file should reveal the tools available to you. As well as the simple expedient of manually turning off message notifications, your software will probably have the facility to set rules whereby messages from certain senders, or those containing particular words, are allowed through or forwarded to another email address which can be set up with automatic notification. Some email software permits the initial downloading of headers only, rather than full messages. You at least reduce the temptation to deal with each message immediately if another action is required before you can read it, and you can usually tell which messages are important from the header information. At the very least you should seek to turn off audible notification of incoming messages and texts. There's nothing more likely to make us interrupt what we are doing than the urgent beep of an arriving message. It is liable to trigger feelings of anxiety or curiosity that may be impossible to resist.

Twenty ways to reduce distractions and interruptions

1 Free yourself from the belief that you have to be constantly connected if you want to work effectively. While there are many benefits to today's instant communication culture, there are equally considerable disadvantages. As noted earlier, effective multitasking is largely a myth. Only by switching off or otherwise limiting sources of interruption for at least part of your working day will you be able to present yourself with the space to carry out tasks requiring concentrated attention.

2 Be clear about what you are trying to achieve in your day. Following the advice on planning and tracking your time in Chapter 2 will help you to rate the importance of distractions and interruptions, and keep your focus on what matters in terms of overall productivity. Additionally, control of your schedule will allow you to deflect would-be interrupters by giving them a clear indication of when you will be available to deal with the issue they wish to raise.

3 Schedule blocks of time in your calendar for occasions when you will deal with those tasks that require uninterrupted concentration and will be unavailable for meetings, calls and other interruptions. Treat this time in the same way as any other scheduled commitment and, with luck, others will come to respect your interruption-free zone.

4 Prepare in advance for your 'do not disturb' periods. Make sure you have everything you need to carry out the tasks you have set and are clear on your aims for the session, so that you can pitch in straight away and make the most of the available time.

5 If you work in an open plan environment and have no other way of signalling times when you don't wish to be interrupted, consider using a 'Please Do Not Disturb' card by your desk. Alternatively, the use of noise-cancelling headphones can serve as both a means of reducing audible distractions, and as a signal that you don't wish to be interrupted.

6 To guard against self-generated distractions, try setting a timer for a specified period (thirty minutes to one hour) and permit yourself no digressions of any description during this interval. Once the stage is complete, allow yourself a five-minute break to do whatever you wish, before setting a further timed period. The penalty for breaking away from task during your planned session is to reset the timer and start again from the beginning of the chosen stretch.

7 Most self-generated interruptions are the result of habitual responses to uncomfortable sensations such as anxiety, boredom or feelings of isolation. Identify the triggers that apply in your case and replace time-wasting habitual responses with more constructive strategies for re-focusing. For example, rather than escaping an anxiety-creating task by engaging in aimless web-browsing or social media activity, take a five-minute walk away from your desk that allows you to calm the mind and return to your main task re-invigorated.

8 Some tasks give rise to a level of anxiety that is out of proportion to their degree of difficulty. Getting them out of the way quickly can free you from a tendency to self-interrupt.

9 Consolidate multiple minor tasks such as sending messages and making phone calls to avoid each one becoming a separate interruption to your workflow. You will handle them more effectively and save significant amounts of time that may currently be spent re-focusing after each interruption.

10 Establish some rules for how frequently you will deal with emails that take account of the culture and expectations in your workplace, but ensure you are not constantly responding on the fly.

11 Take meal and drinks breaks at predetermined times. Build them into a constructive work routine, so that they start to work against self-inflicted interruptions.

12 Help to foster a climate conducive to effective work by treating colleagues as you would have them treat you. Avoid excessive copying or forwarding of unimportant emails to others, and don't expect people to refrain from interrupting you, if you're in the habit of interrupting them.

13 Remember that a cluttered workspace is a potent source of distraction. This applies to your computer desktop as well as your physical space. Remove unnecessary and distracting objects and icons, and perhaps make use of the facility for creating different computer desktops to have one for times of concentrated activity which is stripped of any potentially distracting links.

14 Consider relocating when you have a task that needs concentrated thought – working from home, library or quiet room to avoid everyday workplace distractions.

15 Return phone calls at times when people are unlikely to be keen to enter lengthy conversations – just before lunch, or at the end of the day when they want to get home. Alternatively, set timed calls when agreeing to phone back – 'I've got five minutes to spare between appointments at four o'clock. Can I phone you then?'

16 Give thorough briefings when passing on tasks to others, so that they have less need to come back to you with follow-up questions. Clarify instructions and address any weaknesses in procedures that lead to repeated queries.

17 When carrying out work on the internet, beware of following links that lead you to other interesting but irrelevant material.

18 Consider the use of a blocking app such as Freedom or Cold Turkey, which can allow you to close off access to potentially distracting websites, apps or even the entire internet for scheduled periods.

19 If you have senior colleagues who consider that every summons constitutes a reason for you to drop everything, be prepared to work patiently and diplomatically with them to improve awareness of the effects of their behaviour. Share with them, at times other than when they are interrupting you, the measures you are taking to manage your day, and demonstrate the effectiveness of your strategy by your results.

20 Overestimate the time you may need to complete a task, so that people don't start to chase you prematurely.

Minimizing disruption

When interruptions are unavoidable, aim to reduce their impact on your workflow.

1 When interrupted during a demanding activity, jot down a quick note or some key words that will help you more readily pick up again from where you left off. When you do return to the task in hand, be prepared to briefly revisit what you were doing immediately before the break in order to tune back in.

2 Stay in control of the interruption. If the matter appears complex, offer to phone the person back, or meet them later rather than trying to deal with it immediately, and give an indication of when you will be available to do that.

3 Put a time limit on interruptions. Let the person interrupting you know that you can only spare, say, five minutes. Some experts suggest keeping an egg timer on your desk and using it to remind your visitor to get to the point quickly.

4 Appear unavailable. Position office furniture and desk to avoid giving your working area a 'please walk in and sit down' appearance. This is particularly important if you are in an open-plan office. Risk being considered rude by not inviting interrupters to sit down.

5 Encourage visitors to come with a bullet point note of what they want to talk to you about. This helps you to tune into the issue quickly, helps them to focus their thinking, and deters more frivolous interruptions because of the preparation involved.

Aim to achieve flow

At the other end of the scale from the 'continuous partial attention syndrome' that afflicts many of our working lives is the highly productive state commonly described as flow. This is characterized by absolute focus on the task in hand to the exclusion of both internal and external distractions. If you have experienced this condition, you surely will be able to testify to the sublime sense of almost effortless activity in which all your expertise is unfailingly directed towards the task in hand and where successful performance proceeds almost without conscious input from yourself. Achievement of a flow state is most commonly associated with creative activities such as art, music and writing, but it can apply to any high-level activity requiring skill, expertise and commitment. You're unlikely to achieve it when engaged in a low-level task you find boring, but in those activities that require extended concentration and full employment of your skills it's a most worthy state to aim for. What's more, it has been shown to impose more limited demands on our mental resources than the unproductive and less enjoyable state of constant distraction.

The first precondition for achieving flow is relaxation. You have no hope of getting there if you are anxious, stressed or flustered. Many experts recommend a preparatory focusing exercise that combines deep relaxation with total immersion in the present moment, freeing you from thoughts of past or future. Those who have experienced mindfulness training will be familiar with such routines. You must allow the task to monopolize your complete attention, any tendency to flit or multitask will stop flow in its tracks. Needless to say, a significant period of uninterrupted time is also a necessity, as is a comfortable environment free from external distractions. If your work is normally computer based and you are inclined to fall prey to distractions such as casual browsing and email checking, you might want to consider using an additional local user account stripped of the diversions normally present.

You can't force yourself into a state of flow, and it won't always happen for you, but if you create the right conditions and, importantly, maintain your belief that it is something you can achieve, then you should find yourself increasingly able to enter this most productive state of mind.

Activity – ask yourself

What measures do I intend to introduce in pursuit of fewer distractions and interruptions? List your responses and decide which measures you will implement immediately and which you will bring in at a later date.

Learn to say 'no'

A large part of organizing yourself is about remaining in control of your workload. If you always say 'yes' to requests that come your way, then you lose that control. You over-burden yourself, with the resultant stress, and by saying 'yes' to unimportant requests you may find yourself unable to fulfil key objectives. There are a number of reasons why saying 'no' may be difficult:

- You don't want to appear unwilling and spoil your prospects.
- You're concerned that you might displease others or hurt their feelings.
- You underestimate the increased pressure you will be under as a result of saying 'yes'.
- You simply don't realize that saying 'no' is an option.

Of course, you don't want to get a reputation for negativity – a knee-jerk 'no' may be worse than a knee-jerk 'yes'. If you are in the process of establishing yourself in a new job or interest group, you may need to say 'yes' more often than is good for you. But it is important to be able to draw the line skilfully and assertively, and recognize that it is impossible to please everyone all the time. Decide which requests you need to turn down by asking yourself:

- How does this fit with my main objectives?
- Will my prospects be affected if I don't do it?
- What else might I need to drop or postpone in order to undertake this? What will be the effect of that on other objectives?
- Will doing it result in any detrimental lifestyle effect – significantly increased stress, unreasonable intrusion on my leisure time?
- Will I miss out on any opportunity to develop a new skill if I don't do this?

Try a balance sheet approach – pluses on one side, minuses on the other – where the choice is difficult.

How to do it

There are three ways of approaching 'no'.

Aggressive approach

Complains loudly about being overburdened and taken for granted. Accuses the person making the request of being unreasonable, rants or bursts into tears.

Timid approach

Responds to the request with mumbled attempts to delay a decision. Leaves the person making the request unclear about whether 'yes' or 'no' has been said. Wastes energy fretting about the request and ends up doing it resentfully.

Assertive approach

Indicates pleasure at being asked, but explains succinctly and politely why he or she is unable to respond positively. Suggests possible alternative ways of getting the task done, and specifies what support he or she can offer to whoever takes on the task.

Needless to say, the third is the approach you should aim for. The person making the request is under no misapprehension about your response or the reasons for it, but does not come away from the encounter angry and brow-beaten; and you do not damage your reputation for helpfulness and positive thinking. Often it is fear of confrontation that leads us to say 'yes' more frequently than we should. The technique of visualization, introduced in Chapter 2, can help in preparing for potentially difficult encounters.

When faced with an unexpected request or put on the spot for an immediate response, it can be difficult instantly to weigh up the pros and cons of the proposition, and there may be an inclination to answer yes to something you might later regret. In such circumstances ask for time to consider the request, and give your reasons; for example, the need to take account of its impact on your overall workload. If you're dealing with a reasonable person, they will hopefully recognize the validity of your request and agree to a deferred response.

Take particular care with requests where the commitment asked of you is not immediate, but comes at some time in the future – a request to make a presentation at a conference, for example. When the event is three months away, it's easy to be over-optimistic about the time you will have to fit in the necessary preparation. But as the day approaches and you find your schedule ever more crowded, the additional task assumes the status of an unwelcome addition to a heavy workload, and you end up resentfully turning out a rush job which doesn't do you justice. Awareness of priorities, clarity about your schedule and control over planning are the ways to ensure that you don't fall into this trap.

Activity – ask yourself

What situations and individuals within my workplace should I aim to deal with more assertively? How might I prepare for delivering more assertive responses?

Summary points

You can achieve greater effectiveness in those aspects of your work that involve others by:

- helping to ensure that the meetings you attend are as productive as possible;
- delegating in the right way and for the right reasons;
- actively working to beat distractions and interruptions;
- learning to say no assertively.

06
Organize your space

The way you organize your space can have a considerable effect on your productivity – saving time, preventing fatigue, allowing you to complete tasks more quickly. But it's very easy to become accustomed to a working environment that is less than ideal, and it makes sense to review the ergonomics of your workspace from time to time. You might ask yourself questions such as the following:

1 Is there space and absence of clutter on your desktop to allow you to work comfortably and without distraction?

2 Is there space adjacent to your computer for any papers you may need while you are working at it?

3 Do you have a suitably adjustable and supportive chair?

4 Is your office furniture best positioned for your different needs – working at your desk, using the computer, meeting with colleagues or customers?

5 Are those accessories and items of equipment you use regularly accessible when you need them? Have an eye to the changing nature of your job. It's quite often the case that we leave reference books or items of equipment in easily accessible places long after they have ceased to be vital parts of our daily routine, while other things that have assumed greater importance are left out of reach.

6 Are your cupboards, drawers and bookcases crammed with items you don't need?

7 Is your storage equipment appropriate for the items you need to keep in it?

8 Are computer monitors appropriately positioned? Are they at the right height (top of the screen no higher than eye level), not subject to reflected light or extremes of contrast, and at a suitable distance to prevent eye and neck strain?

9 Are you able to maintain a comfortable and balanced posture for keyboard use, with your forearms, wrists and hands in a straight line and without the need to rest your forearms or wrists on sharp edges?

10 Would it pay to address issues associated with extensive laptop or tablet use? Both tend to foster a crouching posture that can lead to back and neck problems. If you use a laptop as your main computer, you might consider a separate keyboard and monitor.

The importance of movement

Recent research has emphasized the importance to our health of regular movement. Simply put, many of us spend far much far too much time crouching over our computers and it is claimed that our general health will benefit significantly if we simply stand up every 15 minutes or so. And what is good for our general health also makes a difference as far as concentration and motivation are concerned. Standing up and walking about regularly can play a significant role in keeping us on track.

It seems there is also a psychological element to working while standing. We tend to feel a greater sense of urgency to complete the task in hand and are less liable to be distracted than when seated. Survey participants report improved focus and reduced temptation to flit from one task to another.

For those wishing to introduce a greater degree of standing activity, there are numerous standing workstations available, as well as height adjustable monitor and keyboard stands that will allow you to adapt an existing desk. Of course, excessive standing in one position can bring its own health problems, and switching between standing and sitting through the course of the working day has to be the best option. You might consider standing for certain tasks such as making phone calls, reading documents on paper or tablet and dictating correspondence using voice-recognition software.

Tackle disorganized workspace

Disorganized workspace is a potent source of wasted time and unnecessary stress. Tackling it is a tangible commitment to a more effective way of working. The area on and around your desk is the most important part of your working environment, and you might be tempted to tackle it first. But I suggest that you begin by clearing cupboards and drawers, in order to free up space to accommodate items that are cluttering your immediate desk area.

Organizing cupboards, drawers and bookcases

These are all handy hiding places for things you don't need. Start by looking at the cupboards furthest away from your desk – they are likely to have the greatest proportion of redundant material, untouched by previous purges – and move inwards towards your desk. That way you will always have space to house items that are currently jamming up more immediate working areas. Clear out the junk ruthlessly. If there are items that really cannot be discarded, but hardly ever need to be looked at, put them in archive boxes or another long-term storage facility. Remember to take a note of the box contents and file it where you will be able to find it.

Work through all your cupboards and drawers, discarding junk, grouping like items together and making sure that items such as box files are clearly labelled. With bookcases it helps to take everything out before rearranging according to subject matter. The fact that books come in stubbornly different sizes means that you won't be able to achieve perfect organization, and you shouldn't waste time trying. All you are attempting to do is organize material so that you can quickly put your hand on it when the need arises.

Organizing your desk space

For all the explosion of electronic communication in recent years, many of us still have to deal with large quantities of printed material in our working lives. I used to pretend that I could work well with a cluttered desk. Despite the various piles of paper, at times threatening to engulf the workspace, I claimed that I could easily put my hand on any document I needed and that shifting my attention from one task to another kept me sharp throughout my working day. It was nonsense, of course. Superfluous papers are a distraction from the job in hand in much the same way as interruptions and phone calls. It is all too easy to flit around a crowded desk, pecking at tasks rather than devoting the concentrated effort needed to complete them. The presence of a multiplicity of documents is also an excuse for procrastination. When you are struggling with one task, it's the simplest thing in the world to shift your energy and attention to another, seemingly more straightforward chore which beckons from the top of a nearby pile.

Searching can waste considerable amounts of time and throw up further distractions. Just consider the number of times you need to root through the piles when a request or phone call summons the presence of a particular piece of paper. Surveys have suggested that 15 minutes a day is a fairly conservative estimate. It doesn't sound much, does it? But when you consider that 15 minutes a day is equal to a week and a half out of every year, the waste of your time is much more apparent. What could you do with that time? If you are disorganized to the extent that you spend 30 minutes a day searching for things, then the reward for greater discipline could be almost three weeks of additional productive activity.

Desktop disorganization also destroys your ability to set priorities. Within the same pile there may be scribbled notes, half-drafted reports, important letters and complete junk. All share a common fate – their importance is only considered when they come to the top of the pile or force themselves on your consciousness in the course of a search for something else.

And then there is the sheer inefficiency of it all. When you start a new task you have to clear some working space, pushing previously incomplete activity into yet higher piles. The same items pass through your hands numerous times, surfacing and resurfacing from the confusion of papers. You waste energy on things that should have been discarded the very first time you saw them. You miss deadlines because the papers that would remind you of them are buried under heaps of other stuff. You even find yourself sorting through the waste paper basket for that important piece of information you remember scribbling on a scrap of paper, which might have been the one which made no sense to you when you picked it out of the pile this morning.

Finally there is the stress. All the time that your untackled paperwork is an amorphous mass, it represents a potent source of disquiet. You are not entirely sure what lurks within those piles and they remain an ever-present reminder of your failure to get on top of your job. Very often the awareness of tasks to be done is more stressful than actually doing them.

So are you convinced? Sure. All that remains now is to do something about it. Use the following pointers to establish a greater degree of order.

- Don't permit loose papers or unregulated piles on your desk. I would recommend the use of three stackable trays. The first for items you have yet to deal with, the second for items on hold that you need to revisit and the third for items you have dealt with, but have yet to file. Ensure that each retains its original function and that none are allowed to develop into general heaps.

- Have an easily accessible rubbish bin and make more use of it than the paper trays.

- Do away with information scribbled on scraps of paper and sticky notes. Replace them with a single notebook.

- Banish excessive personal nick-nacks. Accessories and equipment on your desktop should consist of items you use daily. Other things may be kept close to hand but away from your main working surface. Give yourself plenty of space to work. There is a psychological advantage to the absence of clutter as well as a physical one.

- Build a desk-tidying habit at the end of each day.

- If the current state of your desk presents a major challenge, use the suggestions in the upcoming section on eliminating paper piles to establish a greater degree of order. You may need to overcome a mental hurdle in clearing your desk. There is a tendency to associate a crowded desk with a busy owner, and we all like to think of ourselves as busy. Remember, however, that you can be busy but incompetent and unproductive.

Don't neglect your computer desktop

Just as with your physical desk space, you should be concerned to eliminate clutter that impedes your computer use. A cluttered computer desktop can be a potent source of distraction and make it more difficult to find the things you need from day to day. The unfortunate practice of saving downloads, photos, screenshots and individual files to the desktop can quickly get out of hand, and may be compounded by new installations or upgrades of software which also drop additional icons onto the desktop by default. If you are afflicted by computer desktop clutter, the following pointers may well assist you in becoming more productive.

1 Use designated folders – documents, photos, downloads – for storing new material and organize them in accordance with the advice in Chapter 7.

2 Screenshots may be saved to a folder of that name or, often more helpfully, put together with other relevant material in an application such as OneNote or Evernote (see Chapter 8).

3 Pin those applications you use regularly to the Task Bar or use the Start Menu to launch them. Get rid of unnecessary shortcuts on the main desktop screen and delete redundant apps.

4 If you feel you must have a multiplicity of icons on your desktop then you might consider using a desktop organization application such as Fences (Windows), Declutter (Mac) or one of numerous, often free, alternatives.

5 Only put files that you are working on or temporary files on your desktop, and be diligent about either removing them or sending them to a permanent storage location once you have completed the task in hand.

6 Use the sophisticated search facilities on today's computers to locate items you may have mislaid rather than taking the 'safe' option of keeping them on the desktop.

7 Choose a soothing and pleasant wallpaper image that you won't want to cover up with icons.

8 Use the facility for creating multiple virtual desktops in Windows 10 and Mac if you want to overcome the clutter and confusion that can occur when several applications are open simultaneously.

9 Use the 'recent', 'quick access' or 'timeline' options in your operating system or applications to return to files you have been working on recently.

10 Revisit your computer desktop on a regular basis and remove any build-up of clutter.

Eliminate paper piles

For all the relentless march of technology, many of us still handle significant quantities of paper, and the prospect of tackling the heaps that have built up around your office may be intimidating, but by setting aside some time for a disciplined blitz, you can get rid of them and lift the mental weight of their presence. In addition to items which need action on your part or should be directed to others, it is likely that your paper piles will consist of documents (reports, periodicals, etc) which you have put aside to be read later, items which have not made it to the filing cabinet, and things which you were not sure what to do with.

Your objective is to get through the paper piles; you must not let yourself become bogged down. So, be prepared to attack the offending heaps and deal quickly and decisively with their contents (Figure 6.1):

- **Earmark four empty folders, filing trays or baskets and mark them: Deal with, Distribute, Read, File.**
  Make sure you have sufficient sturdy plastic bin bags for the most important category – the discard pile.

- **Approach the task with the view that the majority of items are destined for the bin.**
  Whatever relevance they had when they joined the pile is likely to have diminished. Don't repeat previous indecisiveness. If in doubt, throw it out.

- **Don't waste time reading items.**
  Skim them to the point of determining whether they are needed and if so put them in the relevant tray or basket.

- **Don't file or act upon things as you go; you will become bogged down and distracted.**
  By all means mark items to assist your actions and filing later, but keep to your main objective – to blast through the pile.

- **Zip through magazines and periodicals.**
  Tear out the pages containing articles you wish to keep and throw the rest away. Don't stop to read any of them at this stage.

Figure 6.1 Eliminate the paper piles

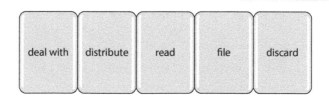

| deal with | distribute | read | file | discard |

- When you have worked your way through the piles, turn your attention to the four trays.
Schedule time to deal with the reading and filing tasks, and use a 'bring forward' system with a concertina file or reminders in your information management app to determine when the 'deal with' items will be actioned.

Tackled in this way, a fearsome chore can become a real stress buster.

Keeping your workspace organized

OK, so you've managed to sort the contents of your office. The things you use regularly are close at hand, you have ditched the junk and cleared the piles. How do you keep it that way?

The answer is, I'm afraid, a boring one. It has a lot to do with developing positive work habits:

- Move paperwork quickly in line with the five Ds outlined in Chapter 4.

- If in doubt, throw it out!

- Don't use your desk as filing space – use project folders or 'bring forward' files for work in progress.

- Keep your equipment needs under review. Are the items you use regularly still in the most accessible places?

- Don't transfer piles of paper on your desk to piles of paper in other parts of the office.

- Try to file on a daily basis. When you remove items from your filing cabinets, make a practice of re-filing them as soon as possible.

Clear clutter at home

Everything that has been written about organizing your workspace applies just as much to your home. If you're living amid clutter it will affect your ability to do the things you want to do, both in work and leisure terms. And a cluttered home is even more common than a cluttered workspace – we have a psychological attachment to many of the things that we bring into our homes and can display a surprising degree of reluctance to discard items that have long since outlived their usefulness. What's more, around the home there tend to be lots more places where clutter can accumulate.

Clutter isn't just unsightly, it's a potent source of wasted time. The list of things we spend time looking for around the home can be quite lengthy: tools, utensils, stationery items, keys, books and magazines, clothes and shoes, letters, bills and receipts, DVDs, directories and address books. You may even think of some additional categories that apply in your own case. Take a moment to ask yourself what are the main items you spend time looking for and what are the reasons you regularly misplace them. Could it be because they don't have habitual storage locations to which they are routinely returned? Or is it because the items concerned are simply overwhelmed among lots of other clutter that should have been discarded? You might like to conduct an audit of your own situation over a period of days as a way of galvanizing yourself into action.

So, how do you bring some organization into your home space to accompany the steps you have taken in your work area?

You can start with a similar sort of blitz to the one I described earlier in relation to office workspace, but don't try to tackle the whole house at once. Take it a room at a time. Once again separate items into four categories, but this time make them: items to keep, items to store, items to donate to the charity shop and items to ditch. Be particularly ruthless with the 'items to store' category. Rather like paperwork filing, you can be pretty sure that most of the things you pile into the loft will never be needed again.

I need to acknowledge that often there is a significant psychological barrier to be overcome in this process. It's the 'you never know when it's going to be needed' hurdle and I'll admit to having been affected by it. It's important to be tough with yourself in challenging that 'might just be needed' assumption and only give in to it in the most compelling of circumstances.

Once you have decided what you are going to keep, make sure there is a suitable home for everything. Magazines that go back into a pile will start the clutter cycle all over again. Work hard over the next three or four weeks at returning items to their proper place until you have built up a regular habit. While you're achieving this, it's a good idea to have a mini purge at the end of each day, putting things away. Just as with your workspace, take care to house the things you use frequently in the most accessible locations.

Ensure that you have suitable storage for the things you are going to keep. A filing system that you habitually maintain for essential paperwork is often just as much a priority in the home as it is in the office. Stackable storage boxes can be useful for those objects that aren't readily housed in drawers or cupboards. Just make sure that you label them appropriately and keep like items together, so that you don't have to rummage through the lot whenever you want a single item.

There will always be some items that are difficult to categorize, and even the most organized households tend to have a miscellaneous junk drawer somewhere. While you can't hope to eliminate this entirely, it's important to check its contents from time to time with a view to deciding whether items might usefully be grouped with others elsewhere.

In working to build up an organized habit, pay particular attention to the places where things tend to accumulate – the kitchen table for example, or by the front door. Make a rule that for every new item of furniture or equipment you acquire, you will get rid of something. With items that you have in multiple numbers, ask yourself seriously how many you really need, and get rid of those surplus to requirements.

Activity – ask yourself

What should be my priorities in terms of organizing space?

1 Furniture and equipment layout and ergonomics.

2 Disorganized storage and desk space.

3 Clutter at work and at home.

Identify the issues to be dealt with in order of importance, and include them in your master 'to-do' list.

Summary points

The key aspects of organizing your space are:

- arranging your furniture and equipment to maximize safety, comfort and productivity;
- freeing up time and space by reorganizing your desk and storage space;
- reducing stress by eliminating stacks of paper around your office;
- tackling the clutter around your home.

07
Organize filing systems

Not many years ago, a chapter such as this would have been all about the physical storage of paper documents. Today, we need to take account of the sheer amount of information that never finds its way into print – emails, web pages, shared electronic files – as well as the options for electronic storage of paper documents. We'll look at the latter towards the end of the chapter, but first let's consider the organization of files that reside on your computer or in cloud locations that you control. Note that the provision of company-wide centralized storage is an issue beyond the scope of this book.

Organizing computer files

You might feel that, with all the sophisticated file management and search tools now available, attention to organizing your computer files is unnecessary. For users of recent operating systems, the entry of a single word or phrase in the search box of the Start Menu is sufficient to throw up an instant list of all the files containing that term. Nevertheless, I would still strongly advocate a simple and logical grouping of material into folders and sub-folders. It takes very little time to do, it makes tasks like archiving more straightforward, and there will be occasions when it is easier to go to a sub-folder where you know you can locate a file than to attempt recall of a name or keyword in order to run a search. Furthermore, if you're creating a lot of files with similar content, then desktop search may not be a great deal of help to you.

Needless to say, you should start by ensuring that the files you have created are separate from any program files on your computer. Using the 'Documents' facility provided by your operating system makes it easier to locate them, to back them up and to prevent accidental erasure.

I suggest that you then decide what will be your top-level document storage directory. It wouldn't be helpful for me to be too prescriptive on this as the best arrangement will depend on the nature and volume of your work. My preferred approach is to create a new main folder each year for common document types (word processor, spreadsheet, presentation, etc) as this allows for easy archiving and prevents subdirectories of routine documents getting out of hand. However, the nature of my work is such that I create a limited number of quite large documents and, for those with a high volume of files, a different balance between current and archive folders is likely to be in order. Many prefer to make groupings such as 'customers' 'suppliers' 'projects' the top-level destinations and to shift files related to completed work regularly to similarly named archive folders. Whatever your choice you will want, within your main directories, to set up subfolders that provide homes for the different categories of activity and types of routine document you create.

Once you have arrived at the most logical grouping of documents to meet your needs, it's important to stick to the system. If you find yourself with an overly large number of subfolders within a folder, you may need to consider splitting it or indexing the subfolders in some way.

The business of choosing filenames is all about simplicity and accessibility once again. It greatly helps to have filenames that mean something to you when you seek them out. You don't want the irritation and wasted time of opening a file only to find that it is not what you thought it was. If your software automatically offers a filename based on the headings used for the document, this may sometimes be adequate, but frequently such names are overly lengthy and you should take care if you're producing a number of documents that have similar headings. Documents such as letters or meeting notes may be best saved with a name and date (the YYYY/MM/DD format ensures that they will be arranged in date order – eg Bloggslet20221215 or Safetymtg20220326) so that other documents relating to the same person or meeting can be easily identified. Of course, where you are likely to create a large number of documents related to the same subject, organization or individual, it makes sense to group them within a sub folder. For projects, it is generally helpful to have files of all types – word processing, presentations, spreadsheets – within the same folder.

Don't try to save everything. Computer files are a great deal easier to store and retrieve than paper ones, but unnecessary saving can result in jumbled folders with consequent difficulty in finding the items you want. It usually makes sense to get rid of rough drafts and working documents that you have stored on the way to producing major pieces of work, and keep just the final version. However, if there is a good reason for keeping some working documents, make sure that they are clearly identified as such.

Delete unnecessary emails and keep only those that require further actions or contain information you may need in the future. Create folders for the emails you are going to keep and make a habit of routinely filing them rather than leaving them jamming up your inbox. Set up archiving arrangements so that current folders are cleared of old messages at regular intervals. Review browser favourites and saved web pages too. They are just as liable to become out of date.

Manually filing paper documents

Regardless of how technically geared up you are, it is likely that there will continue to be some documents you will keep in paper form. They may be working papers related to current activity, original hard copy that it is sensible to keep for legal or taxation reasons, or items that it would simply be too much of a hassle to digitize and store electronically. In some areas of work, storage of documents in paper form is still very much the norm.

Up to 85 per cent of the material stored in the average filing cabinet is never referred to again. That means, for every five documents painstakingly categorized, punched and filed, possibly just one will be needed in the future. And the chances are that the one that is needed will prove frustratingly difficult to locate. It's a case of the 85 per cent you don't need getting in the way of the 15 per cent that you do.

It is difficult to predict with certainty those documents you will need again. Some things do need to be stored on a 'just in case' basis, but you can drastically cut down on the chore of filing and failure to find the documents you need by more confident use of the 'discard' option when you first receive material. Filing is not a matter of getting a document off your desk when you're frightened to throw it away, but are not sure what else to do with it. A document should only be stored when it cannot be readily accessed elsewhere and there is a clearly arguable chance that it will be needed again in the future.

If you can step away from a defensive filing mentality – better save it, just in case – to an attacking frame of mind, then you have much more chance of getting yourself a lean, mean filing system that works for you. For every document you consider filing, ask yourself 'What use will this document be to me in the future?' If you don't get a convincing answer, ditch it.

In addition to defensive filing, there are a number of other common document storage problems. How many of the following apply to you:

- Inappropriately located information?

- No structure to the filing system, or a structure which hasn't been kept to?

- Insufficient thought given to the appropriate grouping of items to allow for easy retrieval?

- Failure to weed out obsolete material?
- Forgetting what files you already have and setting up folders which duplicate existing categories of information?
- Filing material that is easily accessible elsewhere?
- Setting up too many categories within a system so that it becomes unmanageable?
- Use of inappropriate storage equipment for particular types of material (eg suspended files straining to hold weighty reports and periodicals)?
- Time spent searching for things which have been misfiled?
- Indecision about where to put things?

Your choice of location and storage medium should take account of the frequency with which you may need to consult files.

Current projects and activities

These are files which you may need to consult several times in the course of a day and so should be kept either in desk filing drawers or in a filing cart immediately next to your desk. As well as files for individual projects or assignments in progress, you may want to earmark a file each for correspondence pending, reading and meetings. They can help you to avoid the tendency to put things back into your in tray or to create piles on your desk. If you choose this approach, you need to take care that these files don't become general dumping areas. 'To read' files are particularly prone to this. General files may also result in date-related information being overlooked – preparatory reading for a meeting, for example, or a letter that needs to be answered by a particular date. Use a concertina file with a 'bring forward' system to overcome this problem.

Main reference files

Your main filing system is for the things you need to refer to from time to time. Material from the current projects and activities category will find its way there provided it is worth keeping. Don't simply transfer current project files to your main filing cabinet when the project is completed. Very often they will be cluttered with working papers and rough drafts that are of no further significance. Ruthlessly weed out the junk if you want to be able to lay your hands on the important stuff.

Setting up a manual filing system

First decide on broad divisions in which you want to group your files. These will clearly depend on the nature of your work, but examples of category titles might include: clients, staff, projects and administration. You might like to consider colour coding files within each category, so that when seeking a file you can quickly go to the right part of the cabinet. This is particularly useful when you are using a lateral filing system rather than a drawer filing cabinet. Alphabetical order is normally the most convenient arrangement for individual files within a category.

In deciding the titles for individual files, choose the broadest possible description consistent with manageability. You will want to avoid the need to split overlarge files within a short time and, equally, will not want to find yourself with lots of files each containing just a few documents. Neither is conducive to easy retrieval, which is the sole reason you are engaged in the task. If your file headings are too broad, then you might as well leave the documents in piles. Don't try to predict all the files you may need in the future – you'll end up with some empty folders if you do – but remember that your system needs the capacity to expand rationally, so allow space within files and sections for it to do so. Keep titles short and simple, and try to avoid descriptions that are vague or woolly. Miscellaneous files are notorious black holes that are tricky to slot into existing categories, but over time their contents are often able to be grouped into new categories, and so it's important to review them regularly, splitting them and creating new files as necessary.

Choose storage which is appropriate for the material. Use magazine files or box files rather than hanging folders for bulky reports and periodicals. Consider whether you need to store complete copies of magazines and periodicals. Cuttings take up far less room and it is much easier to find the item you want.

Filing documents

If you are following the information handling procedures recommended in Chapter 4, you will already have weeded out that which isn't worth keeping. Here are some additional pointers to ensure that your paper storage is as effectively managed as possible:

1 Make a note indicating the intended destination file at the top of any document you have decided to file. This prevents you having to reread and decide on destination when you actually come to file the document.

2 If you are uncertain about where to put an item, think about the most likely context in which you are liable to require it in the future.

3 Keep a list of your files handy to help refresh your memory when deciding where to file an item, and to avoid opening new files which overlap with those that already exist.

4 Don't file hard copy of information already stored electronically. Ensure a sensible directory structure for your computer files with reliable back-up. It is quicker to do, easier to find and amend, and takes up less room.

5 Don't file material which is readily available from other sources such as the originator of the document, central archives, internet reference sources.

6 Build up a filing habit. Spending a little time regularly is much less of a chore than trying to wade through a large pile of documents for filing. Try to file daily if possible.

7 If you are tempted to file an item you haven't been bothered to read, ask yourself a very serious 'Why?'

Pruning and weeding your files

Without regular attention, files can rapidly get out of hand. The storage life of material varies hugely – some items become redundant in a matter of weeks, while others need to be kept for years. Weeding out what needs to be discarded or archived can be daunting. If you are working with a file and notice that it contains obsolete information, weed it out there and then, but don't let yourself be distracted from your current task into a lengthy sorting process.

Try to schedule a regular file overhaul. You may opt either for 'big bang' or for 'little and often'. The former is a trawl through all your files, say, every three months. The latter might mean spending five or ten minutes sorting a couple of files at a time. Both have drawbacks. If you're overloaded, the big bang tends to get postponed until a very serious problem builds up. Little and often requires some attention to building up a habit.

However you set about the task, you need to be ruthless with the rubbish and not to allow yourself to become bogged down in spin-off tasks. If there are items which have been misplaced, or one file needs to be merged with another, just put the items where they need to go, and resist the temptation to sort the destination file unless it is one you have already dealt with. Its turn will come in due course.

Digitizing paper documents

Storing documents electronically has the advantage of saving much of the time and space occupied by traditional filing methods, as well as greatly facilitating the sharing of data and retrieval of information. In the case of those working for sizeable organizations there are numerous companies ready to initiate and manage this process, so what follows is applicable only to those such as small enterprises, the self-employed and home users who wish to do their own digitization on a limited scale. The ever-increasing capacity and tumbling cost of the required hardware mean that an electronic filing system is within the scope of any computer user. For really small scale activity you can even do the job with a smartphone, but if you are going to be processing a significant number of documents, it helps to have a decent scanner with an automatic sheet feeder. The necessary software to scan and save your documents will generally come bundled with the scanner, but a relatively inexpensive upgrade or purchase of an OCR package such as OmniPage or ABBYY FineReader will generally add greater sophistication and ease of use. The software you use should allow you to save your scanned documents in any of the major formats including PDF files which, with their compact size, faithful reproduction of text and graphics, and ability to be made searchable, have become the worldwide standard for shared documents.

Making the switch

You shouldn't expect to make a wholesale switch to digital filing casually or immediately. It will take time and planning, and in the initial stages may actually mean more work rather than less. Even with automatic document feeders, scanning remains a chore and not every item comes conveniently in loose sheets. In addition to the items you will always need to retain as paper originals, there may be documents such as bulky bound reports that are simply too much of a hassle to digitize in their entirety. It's inevitable then that for the foreseeable future you will have a dual system, but increasingly those items stored as paper will become the minority. The benefits will start to be seen in terms of greater certainty about what information you hold, less time looking for things, less use of paper, and less space taken up by storage.

For even a self-employed individual it makes sense to plan and phase the switch to digital filing, working from a clear start date when documents of a certain type will be filed this way. For example, you may wish to begin with incoming invoices, and at a later stage move to other forms of documentation. Remember too that there are increasing numbers of documents that will not need scanning because they already arrive in electronic form. Reports, invoices and periodicals that come this way can be filed alongside those you have scanned. If your aim is also to digitize the majority of existing paper files, then you need to take account of the scale of such an operation. It is probably best carried out gradually in conjunction with your regular file review.

Managing your scanned documents

Once digitized, documents can be treated like any other computer files that you have created and stored in your documents library. However, you may want to consider a document management application specifically designed to assist you in managing and retrieving electronically filed documents. A long-standing presence in this field is Kofax PaperPort, which aims at the needs of individuals and small businesses, but there are numerous competent alternatives for organizations of all sizes, offering powerful search and retrieval facilities, assistance with the process of scanning, conversion to searchable PDF files and organization into easily manageable folders, as well as the facility to utilize online cloud storage – allowing users to share documents or access them from a multiplicity of devices.

Storage of documents in electronic form rather than on paper puts greater emphasis on reliable backup procedures. Establish automatic, timed backup to ensure that you are not left with a calamitous gap in your records in the event of a serious computer crash.

Activity – ask yourself

1 What changes to my methods of storing information would help make me more organized?

2 Which of these can I make immediately, and which will need to be postponed for now or brought in over a period of time?

3 Decide on an achievable schedule for proposed changes and enter them in your master to-do list.

Summary points

Effective storage of information requires:

- clarity about what is and is not worth filing;
- a simple and logical structure that is routinely adhered to;
- regular pruning of redundant material.

08
Use technology effectively

Technology may be both an aid to organization and a factor leading to greater disorganization. On the plus side is the fact that it has never been easier to find information we need, to communicate quickly and easily and to carry out tasks to a professional level that previously would have required the employment of specialists. On the downside is the huge capacity of technological applications to present us with constant distractions and interruptions, and of the sheer volume of information from multiple sources to generate overload. It has been estimated that workers in the UK check their smartphones once every twelve minutes on average, and that this along with other manifestations of constant connectedness may in part account for the country's failure to achieve significant productivity gains in recent years. So how do we ensure that we remain on the upside of technology? Well, it has to be about using some of the techniques outlined in previous chapters to cut out the time-wasting elements, while making judicious choices and effective use of the time-saving tools that are available.

Know when not to use technology

Information technology has become so all pervading that one may be tempted to use it for every information handling task.

This would be a mistake. There are occasions when the effort of using technology outweighs the advantage, or the medium is inappropriate:

- setting up a spreadsheet to produce a handful of one-off calculations that could be done quicker and just as reliably on a calculator;

- engaging in excessive internet research before embarking on a creative task, and finding yourself overwhelmed with other people's ideas before you have a chance to formulate your own;

- using email, text messaging or instant messaging in unsuitable situations – for example, interactions requiring sensitivity or subtlety that call for face-to-face or, at the very least, telephone contact;

- using time and energy to learn a software package for a function that could be performed manually and has only marginal or occasional significance in your workload.

Software choices

Computer users and smartphone owners face a multiplicity of choice regarding the tools they might use on their devices. Alongside the established commercial office suites there are open source alternatives, often available free of charge, and options include applications that will reside on the individual's own computer, or may operate online in the cloud. One is frequently spoilt for choice when considering specialist software, and packages range hugely in terms of price and degree of sophistication. Then, among the several million apps available to smartphone and tablet users, there are many thousands devoted to aspects of personal organization. Often the choice of which tool to use will boil down to personal preference between numerous similarly competent products.

The value of a particular package will vary from person to person. It will be dependent on how much you have used other similar products, your level of IT expertise, the way you like to work and the precise nature of your job. More sophisticated is by no means always superior. Often a simple application will meet a need better than one with all the bells and whistles. Many software providers make 'try before you buy' offers even on quite expensive products, enabling you to decide whether a package is right for your needs before committing funds to it. Use magazine reviews and recommendations to aid your decisions, but recognize that only you can make an accurate assessment of whether an application is worth having.

Let genuine needs drive your software decisions. It is all too easy to be enticed by the productivity claims of a particular app or software package, and having acquired it, to look around for a task on which to use it. Using a product to meet an identified need is generally an effective way of learning it, but try to arrive at a realistic assessment of the potential benefits set against the investment of your time in learning to use it.

Deciding to upgrade

Whatever software package or operating system you choose, there is likely to be an upgraded version available within a short time, promising new features and greater effectiveness. Make the decision whether to upgrade by seeking answers to the following questions:

1 Do I need the new features? Few of us use all the features of an application. New ones may sound attractive, but if they don't offer you significant benefits there is no point in acquiring them.

2 Are the advantages likely to be worth the cost and learning investment? Most upgraded packages will be broadly similar to their predecessors, but sometimes a major redesign will require a significant amount of relearning. Improvements may only be marginal, and it can be frustrating to discover that functions you have come to know and use regularly have vanished – spirited away into some unfamiliar menu or even removed

entirely because developers have considered them less useful than the latest enhancements.

3 Will a hardware upgrade be required at the same time? A new or upgraded package may put greater demands on your system, requiring increased memory or processor capacity. Check the minimum specifications before plunging in.

4 Does the package have a track record of reliability? These days software is so complex that despite extensive pre-release testing, it's quite common for there to be bugs and glitches in a new package that can prove very frustrating for the user. There may be incompatibilities that prevent other software from working or cause inexplicable crashes. Many experts recommend waiting until initial bugs have been ironed out before deciding to upgrade.

Useful tools

We have already given some consideration in previous chapters to technology that may assist personal organization in specific areas of activity, but I'm going to give further attention here to applications that might provide organizational or time saving benefits to the average user. Clearly, in the available space I cannot do more than scratch the surface of what is available, and the examples given are but a snapshot of well-considered products at the time of writing. Books have a long shelf life, and any product I write about today may no longer be a leading contender in three or four years' time. In this respect computer applications are like racehorses. Favourites don't always stay ahead of the field, and from time to time unfancied runners come through to snatch the spoils.

Readers will wish to make their own investigations before acquiring any of the products mentioned or similar ones. In the following section I shall briefly consider the scope for better organization through the use of applications that aim to assist general office activity, aspects of time management, the organization of ideas and the management of notes. I'll also look at the various ways by which you might speed up the entry of data to your computer or smartphone.

General office activity

There can be few computer users who don't have at their disposal some form of general office software. Unfortunately, applications such as word processors and spreadsheets have become so ubiquitous that we may be guilty of taking them for granted. They are very powerful tools and most of us don't use them to anything like their full potential. We may tend to ignore some of the facilities that could save us time or enhance our personal organization.

Experienced users may also find that they are locked into ways of doing things that were learned when computers were slower and software less sophisticated, or that the trial and error way in which learning took place has bypassed important shortcuts. A short time revisiting the 'What's New?' summary, help file or manual for the software package or app may pay major dividends. Look for facilities you may have previously overlooked, or that weren't present in earlier versions. Check out operations that may simplify tasks, such as automatic formatting of documents, keyboard shortcuts on commonly used commands, or easy customization of toolbars, menus and templates to meet your particular needs.

Time-management applications

Numerous applications over the years have sought to bundle email, calendar and task-management capabilities into what was frequently referred to as a 'personal information manager'. A long-standing and widely used example is Outlook (Microsoft 365) which is a useful tool, able to synchronize across all platforms and both desktop and mobile devices, although it doesn't have the strongest track record on user friendliness. There are well-regarded alternatives to Outlook, some of them free of charge, and one that fulfils very similar functions for Windows and Mac computers is eM Client (www.emclient.com).

Many choose not to go for an integrated application, reasoning that email may be better served by a single-function product, while task management, often the weakest element in integrated packages, needs to move beyond simple 'to do' lists. As mentioned earlier, your choice on task management is likely to be influenced by the extent to which you are looking for a tool aimed at straightforward individual use or one more geared to team collaboration and complex project activity. There are literally scores of competing products across the full range of this market, offering varying degrees of sophistication and collaborative opportunity. I referred in Chapter 2 to Microsoft To Do, Apple Reminders and Google Tasks as examples of entry-level apps, while Monday.com and ClickUp were given as illustrations of more advanced collaborative tools. However, seeking to categorize such applications according to their capabilities isn't always helpful, as some have fairly basic free versions and considerably more advanced pro options. Of the many that occupy this territory, popular choices include Todoist, which has a good reputation for integration with other software, and Trello, which has a large following among those who prefer a more graphical presentation. At the end of the day it will be down to what works well for you and your colleagues, and choice may be aided by the free trials offered by most providers. Given the variety of products and their evolving capabilities, it may be worthwhile making an internet search to get up-to-date reviews and recommendations.

Prodding and prompting apps

At various points in the book I've referred to applications aimed at fostering better working habits. One I mentioned earlier is Rescue Time, which along with other similar applications analyses your computer use and gives you the ammunition to cut out some of the less productive elements of your day. Then, there are those aimed at keeping you on track and resisting distractions. Focus Booster is a typical example that makes use of the so-called 'Pomodoro technique', originally developed by Francesco Cirillo. It works by means of an on-screen timer which can be set for a relatively short period of concentrated thought and action followed by a break. The default timing is a 25-minute session followed by a five-minute break, although this can be varied by the user. The pro version of this application also allows you to track your time against specific tasks and allocate it to particular projects or clients.

Another group of apps seeks to eliminate the distractions of internet activity – very useful for those of us who simply can't resist a bit of browsing when we really should be getting down to it. Examples such as Cold Turkey and Freedom may be useful for those afflicted.

A third group aims at building and reinforcing new habits by issuing timely reminders. For reasons of immediacy these are mostly found as mobile phone apps, although some have a desktop presence. Typically they allow you to set targets, receive prompts and chart progress. There are loads of them for iOS and Android systems, and you'll find extensive reviews online, and user assessments in the app stores.

Organizing ideas

Getting your ideas into a shape where you can start to make sense of them and plan a way forward is often one of the most difficult elements of a new project, presentation or written assignment. For many of us it involves scribbled notes on jumbled scraps of paper that may not mean a great deal when we come to look at them again. Fortunately, there is a group of applications that can make the task easier.

Mind-mapping software

Mind-mapping software is helpful in the initial brainstorming phase of an activity, allowing you to develop a visual scheme of the topics and subtopics that will comprise it, and to highlight the

Figure 8.1   Mapping your thoughts

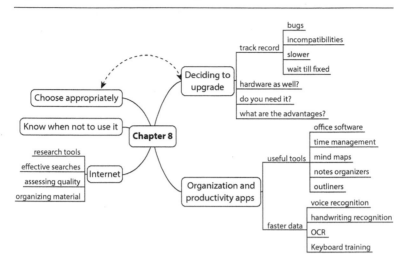

relationships between them (see Figure 8.1). Of course, you can do this on paper, but the value of using a computer application is that topics can be moved, merged and edited, and relationships altered as your thoughts develop, without the need to redraw the whole map. The computer will do the donkey work, leaving you to concentrate on your thoughts. There are numerous mind-mapping applications, both free and paid for. Many have collaborative capabilities allowing them to be used as development tools for teams.

Outliners

Outliners also work with topics and subtopics. They tend to be more structured than those apps in the previous section, and are often useful as a second stage after brainstorming. They allow you to progressively put more flesh on the bones of your document, building up its various levels, promoting, demoting or shifting topics, and collapsing or expanding elements so that you can alternately work upon detail and see the big picture. Some keep the text separate from content so that the outline structure is always visible.

There is a quite competent outliner included within Microsoft Word which often gets overlooked and, as ever, there are numerous other good examples, both freestanding and online, for desktop computers and mobile devices.

Notes organizers

You can use a notes organizer as a form of outliner, gathering together unformed snippets over time and then organizing them into a workable structure. But notes organizers have much more going for them than just outlining, and warrant a section on their own. They are to my mind the most versatile of all tools for organizing thoughts and information from diverse sources in a flexible and accessible manner. Such applications provide you with a ready workspace where you can develop ideas, formulate objectives, build task lists and project outlines or pull together creative activity. They present you with a place to store and index the fruits of your research, including screenshots from websites, notes dropped in from other applications, rough sketches and even elements of audio and video. They offer too a home for all those little bits of information that you want to keep but which don't fit with normal office applications, and which often end up on scraps of paper floating around your desk. There are any number of note organizing packages, but two of the most popular are Evernote and OneNote. Both are available on different operating systems and have the facility to synchronize between devices. With their access to online storage they are also great collaborative tools, allowing members of a team to work together on a document or project plan, with each member's contribution clearly identified.

The applications have different strengths and each has its fans. Evernote is superior in capturing and managing web clippings, and security of storage, while Microsoft OneNote has the edge when it comes to building notes from scratch and organizing them in clear, flexible and intuitive notebooks. It also has the advantage of integrating well with other applications in the Microsoft Office suite. Both have free versions which are able to synchronize between PC, Android and Apple devices, as well as paid for editions incorporating extra features or more online storage.

Rapid input of data

The extent to which you can speedily and reliably input data to a computer, tablet or smartphone, from where it may be manipulated, edited, distributed and stored, is clearly a factor in how well you are able to manage information. If you are a two finger typist, you may well despair of this aspect of your personal organization. Let's spend a few moments looking at some applications designed to help you.

Speech-recognition software

Speech-recognition applications have been around for a couple of decades but have taken off in recent years with numerous smart devices on the market capable of responding to voice commands and requests for information. What I am concerned with here is not so much interactive gadgets as 'speech to text' applications that permit the user to dictate anything from simple emails to lengthy documents and save them to any of the popular office formats, from where they may be further manipulated and edited.

Today's computer, smartphone and tablet operating systems incorporate quite competent speech to text facilities with most processing conducted in the cloud, and have the capability to save resultant documents as text or pdf files. Numerous third party apps are available for both Android and iOS devices, aiming to provide increased flexibility and usability. Speechnotes (www.speechnotes.co) is one well-regarded example for Google Chrome and Android users, while Otter (otter.ai) is a popular transcription tool for both iOS and Android devices.

For those wanting a thoroughly comprehensive product where all the voice recognition processing happens on the host computer I would recommend the market leading Dragon Professional (www.nuance.com). This package, aimed at business users, is fairly expensive, but delivers excellent results and claims to cope with dictation speeds of up to 160 words a minute with 99 per cent accuracy. It permits the input of specialist vocabulary, shortcuts to commonly used passages, and will effectively transcribe to text voice files that have been recorded on other devices, such as digital recorders.

Some speech to text packages may require you to spend a little time training them to recognize your particular speech patterns and correcting a significant number of mistakes before the application becomes used to your voice. And you must continue a firm policy of correcting any errors in words or punctuation that crop up or, rather like an unruly pet, the software will repeat the misdemeanours and become less accurate.

You should remember that dictation is a skill in itself. Many of us have difficulty articulating our thoughts cogently and fluently in a manner that will work well on paper. If you find yourself constantly having to backtrack and amend sections of text, it can remove some of the time savings. And because speech-recognition software works partly by identifying words in context, it prefers speech that is delivered in fluent sentences. Unexpected pauses and any humming and hawing can disrupt its accuracy.

For my part, I find that dictating directly into an application and correcting mistakes as I go along is not very conducive to fluency. When I do this, some of my attention is directed at the accuracy of what I have already said, rather than what I am about to say. I prefer to use a digital recorder and then to transcribe the resulting files to a PC-based package, correcting any mistakes via keyboard and mouse. It's important to do this within the speech-recognition application, as failure to do so will serve to perpetuate the errors.

Optical character recognition (OCR)

I have already referred to OCR in relation to the scanning and filing of documents, but it deserves a further mention here as a technique for rapidly inputting data without the need for retyping.

Competent OCR software will read a printed page and import it to a standard office application – word processor, spreadsheet or presentation package – with all formatting intact. For example, a table of figures can be scanned and dropped straight into Excel with cells accurately filled, and ready to be manipulated in whatever way you require. Pro versions of OCR packages such as OmniPage, ABBYY FineReader and Adobe Acrobat also include useful tools to transfer documents between different formats and turn paper forms into electronic ones.

Quicker keyboard input

Not everyone wishes to dictate emails, and there are circumstances when it may be inappropriate to do so. This is when gesture keyboards come into their own as a means of overcoming the difficulties presented by the miniature keyboards on phones and tablets. Instead of hitting each key individually, you keep your finger on the keyboard and move swiftly from one letter to the next. It takes a bit of practice to get the knack, but once mastered can considerably increase the speed of input on even the smallest virtual keyboards. You do, of course, need an awareness of the keyboard layout to work up a decent speed, so hunt-and-peck typists are likely to find themselves at a disadvantage.

For anyone who feels that their speed and accuracy on a standard keyboard leaves something to be desired, there are numerous online keyboard tutors that, with a few hours' practice, can make all the difference to your skills.

Activity – ask yourself

Take this opportunity to review your current software use, and ask yourself whether there are changes you could make that might assist your personal organization:

- What, if any, applications am I overusing or using inappropriately?

- With which applications that I currently use could I benefit from a review of my work habits in order to make better use of the available facilities and enhance my productivity?

- Are there applications that I do not currently use, but which I believe could make a significant difference to my productivity?

- Which of the above are likely to offer the best payback for the time I may spend learning new techniques or reviewing existing ones?

You might like to draw up a hit list in priority order – headed by those software-related tasks that offer the best payback – and incorporate it into your master 'to do' list.

Organize internet research

The speed and ease with which you are able to access information on the World Wide Web can greatly assist with personal organization, but the sheer volume of information available presents several difficulties:

- separating the information you need from the mass of less relevant data;

- deciding when to stop searching;

- avoiding the distraction presented by other interesting but irrelevant material;

- assessing the quality and reliability of information.

The internet is huge and seductively accessible. You are just a couple of mouse clicks away from billions of pages of information, and the temptation is toward excessive searching, out of fear of missing some vital piece of information tucked away in the vast unruly collection. But resist the urge to seek information perfection. Nowhere does the 80:20 rule apply more than on the internet (80 per cent of the results come from 20 per cent of the effort) and you can waste large amounts of time chasing a rapidly diminishing addition to useful data. Concentrate, instead, on precise and well-planned searches that will get you quickly to manageable quantities of quality information.

Ten tips for effective searches

1 Formulate your search request with care. If you enter keywords that are too general, you risk being deluged with information. Search engines rank responses to queries with those that most nearly meet the search criteria at the top of the list, but a vague enquiry may throw up thousands of responses with similar rankings. Some lateral thinking may be necessary in choosing keywords likely to be in the material you are seeking.

2 Use inverted commas to enclose phrases when you wish the search engine to look for a complete phrase rather than the individual words that comprise it. This can sometimes get you more quickly to information you are seeking, especially when the words within the phrase are common ones.

3 Don't bother to include punctuation, capitals or small words such as prepositions in your search terms. Most search engines ignore them, so they won't benefit your results in any way.

4 Use the plus and minus symbols to narrow down your search. Preceding a search word with the minus symbol will usually exclude any results containing that word from the search, and can be handy for stripping out references unrelated to the information you are seeking. The plus symbol indicates that you specifically want a word included, and is useful when you wish to give a particular word priority or want the search engine to take account of small words that tend to be omitted from searches.

5 Filter by date. It can be very helpful on occasion to restrict your search results to those pages that have been updated recently or within a certain date range. You can do this in Google by clicking the 'Tools' box at the top of the displayed search results, and then selecting a time period from the drop-down menu that is headed 'Any time'.

6 If you are keen to keep abreast of the latest developments in an area of interest, perhaps to stay on top of your work or to keep tabs on the activities of competitor organizations, you might consider Google Alerts (www.google.com/alerts). This gives you access to email notifications when websites that fulfil the search criteria are updated.

7 When presented with search results, don't just start by clicking on those items at the head of the list. Scan the first page or two of results in order to determine which are most likely to meet your requirements. However, don't waste time ploughing through multiple pages of results. If the information you are seeking isn't in the first 100 or so hits, it may be time to re-formulate your enquiry or use more sophisticated tools.

8 Get to know the search engine you use most frequently and take advantage of the advanced search section. These often offer sophisticated filters that may be extremely useful when you're experiencing difficulty unearthing what you require from a standard search.

9 Don't let yourself be distracted by links to other interesting but irrelevant pages. If something attracts your interest, use the bookmark facility to store a record of the location so that you can return to it at a later date.

10 If you need to hark back to a site you have visited recently, viewing your browser history may be an easier option than running a whole new search. The way to access your history may vary slightly, depending on the particular browser and whether you are using a desktop or mobile device. If you're unsure, a quick search should put you right.

Assessing quality

Finding information quickly is all very well, but what about the quality and reliability of what you discover? Within the billions of pages of information on the World Wide Web there is an awful lot of garbage and blatant misinformation. Anybody who wishes can quite simply set up a website or social media presence and present information in an apparently authoritative way. So how do you discriminate between the reliable and the less so? Here are some pointers that may help:

- Is there information regarding the authorship of articles you may be interested in? Does it include such things as contact details, qualifications and relevant publications? In the absence of these, a search on the author's name may throw up helpful information.

- Is the host site that of a reputable body? Generally, at the top of the list for reliability are: universities; national government information sites; local authorities; publicly funded bodies; known voluntary organizations; reputable companies; impartial broadcasters; online versions of respected newspapers and periodicals.

- How up-to-date is the information? Does the web page show a 'last reviewed' date? Are links still relevant?

- Are references given for any facts and figures, research or survey results?

- Are there links to other clearly reputable websites?

- Is there a demonstrable commitment to objectivity in what has been written?

- What is the presentation like? A slap-happy approach to spelling, grammar or presentation may indicate a similar attitude towards the veracity of information.

- Are you able to double-check the information? Similar information on different websites may offer some guide to validity, but take care. Identical or near-identical wording may simply indicate that it has simply been lifted from one site to another.

Organizing the material you find

It's a simple enough matter to download pages for later reference or click on 'add to favourites' to save a link to an interesting or valuable site you may wish to visit again; but if you do a lot of internet research, you can quickly find your favourites list and the file location you use for downloads becoming cluttered and unwieldy. Use 'organize favorites' to set up appropriately labelled sub-folders within the favourites list and drop items from your list into the relevant folder. Similarly, create folders within your page download location that reflect either the subject matter of the downloaded pages or projects with which they are associated. Alternatively, you may wish to use a product such as PaperPort, Evernote or OneNote (all mentioned earlier) which have a useful facility for capturing screenshots of webpages as well as filing and indexing them. Be judicious in what you choose to save – links are generally more valuable than downloaded pages that may rapidly become out of date. It is also a good idea to schedule a regular pruning session to clear out any downloads or favourites that have become redundant.

Activity – ask yourself

What changes might I wish to implement in the way I conduct internet-based research? Rank any points you identify in priority order and enter them in your master list.

Summary points

Modern information technology can be of considerable assistance in personal organization provided it is used appropriately. You need to:

- recognize the tasks for which technology offers no appreciable advantage;
- select software to meet identified needs;
- balance potential time savings against the commitment of time to learn new software applications;
- adopt precise search techniques when seeking information on the internet;
- monitor the quality of information obtained;
- manage and organize any saved material.

09
Organize yourself working from home

In the second decade of the 21st century, the proportion of the workforce operating from home increased considerably, driven by advances in mobile technology and fast broadband, together with an increase in the numbers of self-employed and greater awareness among employers that remote workers can be just as productive as those based in fixed office locations. The global pandemic of 2020 injected rocket fuel into this trend and, at the height of the first lockdown that year, almost 47 per cent of those in UK employment did at least some of their work from home (Office for National Statistics). Numbers have fallen back since then, but nowhere near to pre-pandemic levels, as what was introduced as an emergency measure becomes more of an everyday norm. But working from home introduces organizational considerations not present in more traditional settings and no book on personal organization would be complete without consideration of its advantages and challenges.

Advantages:

- control over your own schedule;
- nobody looking over your shoulder;
- freedom from some workplace distractions;

- flexibility to slot leisure or personal activity into what would traditionally be considered working hours.

Challenges:

- absence of normal workplace structures;
- possible need to juggle different roles;
- potential new distractions;
- absence of boundaries between work and home life;
- communication and cooperation with others;
- possible security issues;
- workspace limitations.

Clearly you will wish to maximize the advantages and overcome the challenges, and all the points made earlier in the book about managing time and understanding the way you work will be of significance. But there are additional issues specific to home-working in respect of balance, focus, security, communication and workspace organization, which we might usefully look at now.

Balance

One of the biggest problems for home-based working is maintaining a balance between work and leisure. You are in control of your schedule, but unless you take care to set and maintain boundaries on your working day, you can find work beginning to invade all your waking hours and, without a degree of discipline, the work you do may not be very productive. With all the trappings of your home around you, there may be a tendency to flit between work tasks and leisure/family activity in a manner that reduces the effectiveness of your work and, because of guilt about neglected work tasks, does not permit full enjoyment of leisure activities.

To maintain a healthy and productive balance between work and leisure, make sure you build a structure to your working day.

What we refer to as normal office hours may feel like a strait-jacket and an unwelcome manifestation of the commuter rat race you have escaped, but they have the benefits of certainty and habit, as well as the knowledge that others are operating to a similar pattern. Schedules are valuable; they put us in the right frame of mind for those things we need to do, and it is arguably even more important to have a firm grip on working times when your schedule is in your own hands than when your hours are dictated by others. One of the most common productivity killers when operating from home is 'morning frittering', where distracting tasks are used to delay getting down to it. There's a bit of cleaning or washing that needs to be done, a spot of gentle web surfing or a magazine article that has just happened to catch your eye. Try to set your start times and stick to them, while also maintaining a predictable schedule through the week.

A pre-work routine that signals the start of your gainful employment is a useful way of getting you into a productive mind-set. It doesn't have to be lengthy, just something that indicates a dividing line between your leisure time and work. Perhaps it's going to a particular location in the house, logging on to a work account or dressing as if for the office. It should mark a change in focus and shake you out of any tendency to waste time. While the idea of rolling out of bed and getting straight down to it in your pyjamas may be an attractive one, many who have made a success-ful transition to homeworking claim that it blurs the lines between work and repose, and is thus destructive of productivity.

There are other milestones in the day that can benefit from habitual routines. Break times may be a case in point. A drink and a sandwich taken at your desk may seem an efficient thing to do, but for some it may hinder the process of recharging and returning to action refreshed. Unproductively extended working hours and consequent burnout are also common among those who operate from home, and a working day closure routine can help combat this. It may be the act of planning your programme for the next day, an exercise session, some scheduled family time or a switch to a pleasurable leisure pursuit that forms a boundary marker and signals a clear end to the working day.

Schedules may be determined to some degree by other members of your household, particularly if you have children, and you need to be mindful of this in planning certain types of activity. You may, for example, reserve high-intensity activity for those times when very young children are asleep or time exercise sessions and snack breaks to coincide with the school run or other family-friendly intervals.

There is, of course, scope for some greater flexibility when working from home and it may be helpful to see your day in terms of core time and flexible time using a broader approach to the common flexitime principle. The core time is that which will always be allocated to work or to family/leisure activity – no excuses, this time is sacrosanct. For example, you might decide that from 9 am until 2 pm every day is core working time and the period after 6.30 pm is core leisure time. The flexible time to make up your working week can move to accommodate a healthy work/leisure balance. One day might involve an early morning start, another some early evening work and a third might follow traditional office hours. Provided you have a significant block of working time that becomes routine and that your family, friends and clients are able to tune into, you can take advantage of the flexibility that working from home offers to improve your lifestyle. It is important that core working hours are impressed on friends and family as there may be a tendency, particularly among those who don't work, to interpret your presence at home as an indicator of unlimited availability.

In structuring your working hours, give attention to the points discussed in Chapter 3 regarding your best times of day for carrying out particular types of activity. You need to focus not only on those core activities that bring in the money, but on the maintenance tasks too: those routine jobs that keep you functioning properly – staying informed, dealing with correspondence and organizing your workspace.

Figure 9.1 Flexible working day

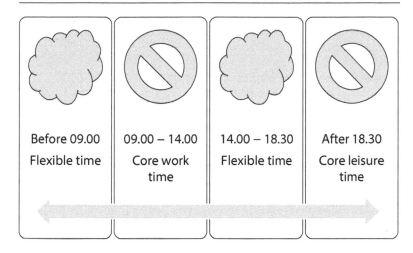

Before 09.00	09.00 – 14.00	14.00 – 18.30	After 18.30
Flexible time	Core work time	Flexible time	Core leisure time

In a traditional work setting, there are likely to be others whose specialist roles support your own. If you are working independently, the chances are that it's all down to you. As well as fulfilling your main role, you may find that you are acting as your own office manager, PA, bookkeeper, marketing executive and odd job person. It may be impracticable or uneconomic to employ others in these capacities, and so you need to find ways by which the full range of activity required for success will be achieved. Rather than allowing tasks to build up until you are forced to have a bookkeeping splurge or a filing blitz, generate a varied work schedule to instil painless habits by weaving the different roles into your daily or weekly routine.

Activity – ask yourself

- What are the various roles I need to fulfil? (List them.)
- Roughly what proportion of my time will be taken up by each of these?

> • How does the market rate for these roles compare with the price per hour that I would put on my time in my main role?

When you are clear about the answers, you might like to consider a formal working arrangement to ensure the necessary services are fulfilled. If, for example, you decide that two hours a week is necessary for bookkeeping you might regard yourself as under contract to provide that service for one hour every Tuesday and Thursday, and approach the duty in just the same frame of mind as if you had been externally hired to fulfil the role. Similarly, you might act as a general administrator for half an hour every day. Visualizing your different roles in this way can help you get to grips with them all and prevent some from being undervalued or overlooked. Putting a price on the various roles also helps you get a handle on those tasks that it might make sense to contract out.

Focus

With a raft of potential distractions around you, working from home presents a greater challenge than the traditional workplace. It's worth recapping here some ideas that should help keep you focused:

1 It's even more important when you're working on your own to plan your activities over different time frames and to break down long-term projects into smaller chunks. It makes tasks easier to handle and gives you that much-needed sense of progress.

2 Keep motivation high by setting yourself tight but achievable deadlines.

3 Stay on top of your schedule by whatever means suits you – paper-based or electronic – but stick to one simple system.

4 Reward yourself for staying on track and meeting your goals.

5 Have clearly defined work locations in your home, especially for those activities that require concentrated thought.

6 Take note of those periods in the day when your energy levels are at their peak and schedule demanding activity accordingly.

7 Consider using checklists of daily and weekly routine tasks so that nothing gets missed.

8 Try strategies such as the Pomodoro technique – limited bursts of concentrated activity (25 to 45 minutes) followed by short breaks of 5 to 10 minutes.

9 Make use of internet blockers such as Freedom and Cold Turkey.

10 Make a rule that emails will only be checked once or twice a day, and stay off social media.

Communication and cooperation

If you are engaged in any form of team activity there will be times when you will need to interact with colleagues in meetings, planning sessions or project work. But the traditional working environment offers opportunities for communication beyond those formal channels and, if you are exclusively operating from home, fostering more casual links with your colleagues may become of greater importance. Many valuable ideas and ways of working emerge from informal interaction, and the mental well-being of those working from home may be heavily influenced by human contact or the lack of it. So, to avoid becoming too detached and insular, try to build informal contact with other remote colleagues or similarly situated self-employed professionals.

More formal links also need to be actively fostered and maintained. It's all too easy for remote employees to slip off the radar of those responsible for developmental opportunities and promotions. Keep abreast of relevant face-to-face meetings and training sessions back at base and make sure you turn up and participate if possible. We all know that meetings can be a colossal waste of time, but they are also opportunities to be noticed, and this applies as much to remote meetings as those that bring all participants together in one room. Try to ensure that you have something useful to contribute and that you aren't simply a silent face on a multi-image screen.

Don't neglect the need for communication and cooperation within your own household. If, for example, there are two or more of you working from home, space may not permit more than one dedicated home office, and it may be a case of you sharing or of hot-desking, with agreement about exclusive office use by one household member for tasks requiring high levels of concentration or privacy. When sharing an office there may also need to be negotiation about the ways in which you like to work. One member may prefer silence while the other likes chitchat and maybe background music. Tackling such issues before they become bones of contention is vital for a harmonious and productive relationship.

Security

Most people today are sharply aware of the need for strict data security in work activity, but in traditional office settings may be inclined to leave its enforcement in the hands of those employed by the organization to maintain it. When operating remotely or in a self-employed capacity the responsibility for data security is no less, but it tends to fall more directly on the individual, and there may be additional complications that arise from sharing workspace and/or equipment with other household members, or the use of that equipment for both work and leisure purposes. It's worth then giving some attention to the particular demands of data security when working from home. Here are a few of the things you may need to consider, but you should seek specialist advice on any matters where you are uncertain.

If the organization you work for has provided you with equipment and software to connect securely with remote networks you should use this exclusively for your work, and take care not to muddle matters associated with your employment with those of your private life. Don't, for example, use a personal email address when communicating work-related matters or a work email address for leisure related activity. Similarly, when using your own equipment and software it's important that you don't mix personal and work data and that you avoid keeping information for longer than necessary. Separate user accounts on your computer for work and personal activity are highly desirable, and wherever possible avoid sharing computer equipment used for work with other household members. If this isn't possible, you should be especially vigilant in protecting the confidentiality of information that might be unintentionally viewed by others.

Protect your work-related information with adequate encryption and passwords, and follow best practice at all times. Too many of us are guilty of choosing easily remembered word combinations, using the same password in multiple situations or failing to change them regularly. You should avoid drawing passwords from personal information, and it is also wise to steer clear of standard dictionary words. The best passwords are those which mix numbers, upper- and lower-case letters and special characters in a manner that is unpredictable for anybody trying to access them. Of course, these are the most difficult passwords to remember, and you may wish to use a password manager – an application that routinely generates high-quality passwords, stores them in an encrypted form, and is able to call them up when needed.

Make sure your Wi-Fi is encrypted and that you have changed the default password for your router. Avoid using public Wi-Fi wherever possible, but if you have to connect, consider using a VPN to do so. Otherwise work offline and connect up once you are back in a secure environment.

We are constantly reminded of the need to be vigilant as far as online threats to our own data are concerned, but an additional layer of responsibility arises when we are handling the personal data of others. Take particular care with website links and attachments to unfamiliar emails. The incidence of scams and phishing attacks continues to rise, so be alive to any indicators that a message might not be genuine and delete it if you are unsure. Maintain effective software that is able to deal with all forms of malicious attack, and ensure that other software on your devices is kept up to date. New threats are constantly emerging, so it's important to initiate regular scans and updates.

The potential vulnerability of personal information in discarded documents is well known. You need to have effective measures in place for the disposal of any paperwork containing your own details and, of course, you have a legal duty to deal appropriately with personal or sensitive information concerning others. The first sensible step towards dealing with this issue is to limit the printing of information as far as possible and you should make sure you have secure storage for any sensitive material that has to be committed to paper. It may be that your main workplace has arrangements for the secure disposal of discarded documents and, if so, you need to be mindful of the need to maintain them securely until such time as you go into the office. If you're thrown onto your own resources for disposal, at least make sure you have a good-quality cross-cut or micro-cut shredder. They do a much better job of rendering a document unreadable than do the cheaper strip-cut shredders.

Appropriate workspace

Attention to good organization of your workspace can give a significant boost to productivity. The idea of firing off emails from the comfort of your bed or mapping out your business plan on a sun-drenched patio may be attractive and, indeed, there may be tasks that you can fulfil comfortably and effectively in unconventional settings, but the likelihood is that for a significant portion of your work some form of office space is a must. Your home office does not have to be grand – forget those extravagant Sunday supplement conversions – but it should be comfortable and functional with attention paid to a layout that suits your working needs. Too often we neglect, in our home-working arrangements, features that we would regard as essential if we were working elsewhere. We give ourselves insufficient or inappropriate space, and use the furniture and equipment that is to hand rather than spending a small amount of time and money creating a working environment that meets our requirements. Take account of the recommendations in Chapter 6 and consider the following fundamental elements:

- **A door you can close when necessary.**
  Working on the dining room table may be convenient, but it presents a packing-up task every time you finish work for the day, and may also render you more open to interruption if other household members are present. Perhaps most importantly, it increases the difficulty of separating working life and home life. Wherever possible your home office should be a single purpose workspace with minimal distractions. Many successful home-workers use a traffic light arrangement or similar to alert other family members when privacy is required. Red circle on the door = Don't disturb. Green circle on the door = OK to come in.

- **A well-proportioned and adjustable chair.**
  Often neglected, this is probably the most important investment you will make.

- **A work surface that is sufficiently spacious to accommodate essential equipment and gives you plenty of free space.**
  It doesn't have to be a fancy desk; there are plenty of inexpensive, well-designed models available, and even foldaway options that could be considered if you are forced to work in a multi function area.

- **A pleasant, well-lit and comfortable environment.**
  Arrangements initially viewed as temporary have a habit of becoming permanent. Take care that you are not making do with inadequate accommodation when a little thought, re-arrangement and minor financial outlay could produce something more conducive to productivity. Working in a dingy boxroom, surrounded by piles of junk, has an effect on your work after a while.

- **Appropriate storage equipment.**
  The items you use regularly should be easily to hand, and the ergonomic/storage advice in Chapter 6 may usefully be revisited. If space is at a premium, go upwards rather than outwards. Shelves, wall-hung baskets and stackable boxes may make up for a shortage of floor space.

There will be other factors to consider, depending on the nature of your work. If it involves clients visiting you, what sort of space do you have to receive them and what sort of first impression will they gain? Would it make sense in some circumstances to choose an external venue for meetings? Are there any local business restrictions or property covenants that could lead to difficulty in conducting your business from home? If a great deal of your work is done on the telephone, do callers always receive a professional response, and might it be worth considering a second landline or mobile number with separate voicemail facilities? This can also be a means of managing potential overlap between work and leisure. Set the work number to receive voicemail during your leisure time and do the same with the home line during your working hours.

There are other issues – legal, fiscal, regulatory – that may come into play with home-working arrangements, particularly if your activities involve the employment of others, premises modification or the setting up of a space to be wholly and exclusively used as an office. But such matters are beyond the scope of this book. There are numerous other books and internet sites offering useful information and advice. Whatever the nature of your home-based work, take the trouble to clarify your needs, research any areas of uncertainty and organize yourself accordingly.

Summary points

When working from home, you should ensure:

- a balance between work and leisure;
- a considered approach to the varied roles you may need to fulfil;
- attention to maintaining focus, communication and security;
- good workspace organization.

10
Keep up the good work

We are all familiar with the phenomenon of resolution fatigue. Good intentions launched with enthusiasm and vigour on 31 December are abandoned and forgotten by 10 January. It's no different with decisions to improve personal organization. Reading this book is a start, but it won't bring all the results you want without some effort on your part.

Review your objectives

In Chapter 1, I invited you to set some objectives in respect of better personal organization, and in a number of reflective exercises you have been encouraged to add to these. Hopefully, you will have made progress as you have worked through the book, and you may consider some objectives to be fully accomplished. It's now time to take stock and address those issues that have yet to move to the top of your agenda, as well as those that may require renewed focus. With the benefit of an overall viewpoint, you may wish to make some amendments to objectives, and you should be in a position to gauge the priorities which various items hold for you. Review your 'better organization' objectives, asking yourself the following questions:

1 Which of these items have already been fully achieved (cross them off)?

2 What amendments, if any, do I wish to make to the remainder?

3 Are there areas of concern that I did not previously identify, but that I now realize require my attention?

Look at your amended list and prioritize the items on it A or B according to your estimate of their value in lifting your current level of personal organization. The priority A items are the most important, the ones to concentrate on first. Set yourself an action plan for them, breaking down each major objective into its constituent tasks together with target dates. If you're carrying out this exercise on paper, you may wish to use a simple table format such as the one shown in Figure 10.1 to assist in drafting your proposals. When you're happy with your action plan, enter tasks into whatever activity tracking system you are using, and get cracking with implementation. You may want to set target dates, but remember my earlier warning about not taking on too much at once. This is especially the case where you need to give new habits time to become established.

Figure 10.1   Action plan

Action plan

Main objective:

Target date:

Sub-goals and tasks	Start date	Target date

Find ways of staying on track

Be on the lookout for any means by which you can keep your objectives at the front of your consciousness and your motivation high.

- Review your progress regularly, weekly if possible, but not less than monthly, and build in regular milestones. There is a corny old saying: 'life by the yard is apt to be hard; life by the inch is a bit of a cinch'. It's certainly true when you are working towards a goal.

- Record your progress. Keeping a diary is a good way of keeping your objectives in sharp focus and delivering valuable reinforcement.

- Give yourself immediate positive reinforcement or reward for every success and use these as stepping stones to further achievement.

- Don't be too hard on yourself when you have failed to achieve the progress you anticipated. Look for the reasons – perhaps you were trying to achieve too many things at once, or maybe you didn't persist for long enough to establish a new habit. Don't let yourself be lured into abandoning your goals, however. Reframe them and move on.

- Visualize the way you will work and the benefits that will accrue when you have perfected new skills and ways of working.

- Make yourself accountable. Working with someone else who is also seeking to achieve important objectives can be an effective strategy. In a spirit of mutual development, each of you holds the other to account for progress towards your goals, as well as providing support and encouragement.

- Share your successes with a trusted friend or partner.

- Adopt novel approaches that work for you. Some people like to place a prominent tick on the calendar for every day when they have achieved all their proposed 'to do' items. Others give themselves points for meeting targets, or deduct them for targets missed.

What if old habits reappear?

You will be very fortunate if you don't experience setbacks in the process of building new, more organized habits. Your old habits are likely to have been acquired over many years, and you can't expect to shift them at the drop of a hat. But setbacks shouldn't be a signal to engage in despair, self-condemnation and abandonment of hard-won gains. We're all a mixture of strengths and weaknesses, and self-development seldom progresses in a straight line. Relapses can even be viewed as opportunities to review, reflect, regroup and plan the next stage of development, armed with knowledge of where the difficulties lie.

Here's what do when old habits start to reappear:

- Examine the reasons why setbacks have occurred. Are they the result of additional burdens, increased stress, out of the ordinary events or simple loss of focus? Whereas some pressures may have been unavoidable, it may be possible to address others so that they don't cause problems in future.

- Don't let the reversals wound your self-belief. Remember that the way you explain setbacks to yourself will very largely determine how you feel about them, and the actions you will take subsequently. Give yourself credit for what you have previously achieved, and use the current adversity to reinforce your resolve.

- Work on the things that are within your control and take a philosophical approach to those that are outside it.

- Revisit your diary. When you are facing a difficult challenge, one of the most valuable things you can have in your armoury is a record of successful development. You can use it to reinforce a problem-solving approach and as a means of building yourself back up from reversals.

- Seek out alternative routes to success where a particular approach is patently not working for you.

- Restate your objectives, refocus on your priorities and recognize that there is generally something to be learned from even the worst experiences.

You can do it!

All the books in the Creating Success series

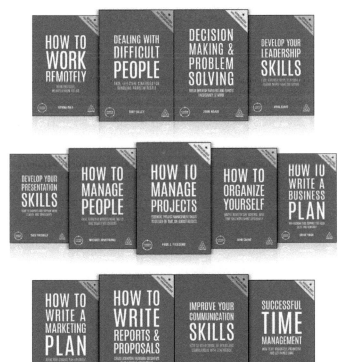